SLEEP APNEA SECONDARY TO PTSD: NEXUS LETTERS FOR VETERANS' VA DISABILITY CLAIMS

Dr. Finnerty examines the controversy and science related to VA disability nexus letters for sleep apnea secondary to posttraumatic stress disorder (PTSD) and other psychological conditions like depression and anxiety. Learn about why nexus letters are sometimes needed in sleep apnea secondary to PTSD disability claims. Dr. Finnerty addresses common reasons why claims are denied and the research supporting a nexus. The book was written both for Veterans interested in researching VA disability benefits for sleep apnea secondary to PTSD and the professionals tasked with helping to determine whether a Veteran's sleep apnea is secondary to PTSD. It is a VA disability claim book related to the medical evidence needed in Veterans' disability ratings.

- The book includes a sample nexus letter from Dr.

Finnerty for sleep apnea secondary to PTSD with extensive research citations

- The book includes commentary from Dr. Finnerty about the VA's proposed rule changes related to how sleep apnea is rated

- A large percentage of denied VA disability claims are later overturned on appeal. The book includes research conducted by Dr. Finnerty to help answer the question *"what are my chances?"* in relation to having a sleep apnea secondary to PTSD VA disability claim approved even after it has already been denied in the past.

Sleep apnea secondary to PTSD: Nexus Letters for Veterans' VA disability claims
Written by Dr. Todd Finnerty

Copyright 2022 Todd Finnerty
Published by NexusLetters.com, an imprint of Todd Finnerty, LLC
ISBN: 978-0-9819955-7-1

Todd Finnerty, Psy.D.
100 E. Campus View Blvd, suite 250
Columbus, OH 43235

http://www.toddfinnerty.com
http://www.nexusletters.com

TABLE OF CONTENTS

ABOUT THE AUTHOR

Dr. Todd Finnerty is a psychologist in private practice. Dr. Finnerty writes nexus letters for Veterans on their VA disability claims and provides independent psychological examinations and DBQ's. He has significant training related to PTSD, including VA-specific training through the contractors VES and QTC. Dr. Finnerty has had the same amount of training or more training than the third-party contractors used by the VA. In the past Dr. Finnerty has performed hundreds of examinations on veterans for VA third-party contractors as a C&P examiner, however now Dr. Finnerty works directly with Veterans or their accredited representatives. Dr. Finnerty also has extensive experience helping to make decisions on Social Security disability claims; in this role Dr. Finnerty was named the 2012 "Disability Review Physician of the Year" by the National Association of Disability Examiners, Great Lakes Region and the 2010 "Consultant of the Year" by the Ohio Association of Disability Examiners. Dr. Finnerty has substantial experience in evaluating impairment. Dr. Finnerty has also received continuing education in behavioral sleep medicine and is a member of the American Academy of Sleep Medicine and the Society of Behavioral Sleep Medicine. Dr. Finnerty is a forensic specialist and adheres to the American Psychological Association's *Ethical Principles of Psychologists and Code of Conduct* as well as the APA's *Specialty Guidelines for Forensic Psychology*. These guidelines include the responsibilities of integrity, impartiality and fairness and note: "When offering expert opinions to be relied upon by a decision maker, providing forensic therapeutic services, or teaching or conducting research, forensic practitioners strive for accuracy, impartiality, fairness, and independence. Forensic practitioners recognize the adversarial nature of the legal system and strive to treat all participants and weigh all data, opinions, and rival hypotheses impartially. When conducting forensic examinations, forensic practitioners strive to be unbiased and impartial, and avoid partisan presentation of unrepresentative, incomplete, or inaccurate evidence that might mislead finders of fact. This guideline does not preclude forceful presentation of the data and reasoning upon which a conclusion or professional product is based." While it would be convenient if Veterans in need of first or second opinions on mental health related claims could seek them from treatment providers at the VA, VA policy outlined in *VHA Directive 1134(2) Provision of Medical Statements and Completion of Forms by VA Health Care Providers* recommends that VA mental health treatment providers not complete forms such as "mental health DBQ's" in order to "maintain the integrity of the patient-provider relationship." Therefore, both the VA and Veterans often must seek forensic specialists like Dr. Finnerty to provide opinions related to their VA disability claims.

ABOUT NEXUSLETTERS.COM

Dr. Finnerty maintains a website at NexusLetters.com where he writes about his services and provides VA disability claim related information for Veterans. Veterans can get a nexus letter from a psychologist based on a records review and/or a psychological evaluation for their disability claim. If Veterans need a mental health diagnosis or otherwise need an exam with a DBQ they can get one through Dr. Finnerty. In addition, Dr. Finnerty writes blog posts and an email newsletter related to VA disability claims. Veterans can subscribe to get information related to Veterans' disability claims sent to their email. There is also a list of other professionals who write nexus letters and/or perform independent examinations for Veterans for referrals and to help Veterans with their research on their claims.

WHAT IS THE PURPOSE OF A NEXUS LETTER?

A nexus is a connection. A Nexus letter is an independent opinion that a medical professional writes for your Veterans' disability case that helps to connect a condition you're currently experiencing with your military service. One way that it could do that is by connecting your condition directly to your military service (this is often referred to as a primary condition). This could be related to an event, injury, traumatic stressor, etc. that occurred while the Veteran was in the military. Another way a nexus letter can be useful is by connecting a current condition to another condition a Veteran has already had service connected (this is typically referred to as a secondary condition). For example, this book addresses nexus letters for independent medical opinions which help to connect a Veteran's currently diagnosed sleep apnea to an already service connected posttraumatic stress disorder (PTSD).

VA DISABILITY SECONDARY CLAIMS

Veterans don't have to show that their condition began while they were in the military and don't have to have medical evidence that their condition existed while they were still in the military. For a secondary condition Veterans have to demonstrate that their condition was at least as likely as not due to or substantially aggravated from baseline by a different condition that was caused by the military. For example, in this instance, veterans need to demonstrate that it is at least as likely as not that their sleep apnea was caused or substantially aggravated by their already service connected PTSD.

SHOULD THE VA CONSIDER A PSYCHOLOGIST'S OPINION IN RELATION TO SLEEP APNEA SECONDARY TO PSYCHOLOGICAL DISORDERS?

Judges and administrative bodies like the VA get to decide who the expert is. Whether someone is considered to be an expert on a particular topic isn't just established by their professional licensure alone. For example, just because someone is a physician assistant doesn't mean they are an expert on all medical and psychological questions under the sun. The credentials, education, training and experience for each specific professional should be considered on a case-by-case basis for the specific question being asked. Professionals offering opinions on sleep apnea secondary to PTSD should be familiar with both sleep apnea and PTSD and the research related to the association between the two. They should not just have basic knowledge about sleep apnea OR PTSD. They certainly shouldn't be called upon as an expert if they have only a basic understanding related to sleep apnea, no significant expertise in PTSD and haven't done a sufficient literature review related to the research connecting the two. Likewise, the VA has the ability to consider whether the opinions from a specific professional are consistent with the evidence and reflect competent medical evidence for the purposes of a VA disability claim. Per the VA: *Competent medical evidence means evidence provided by a person who is qualified through education, training, or experience to offer medical diagnoses, statements, or opinions. Competent medical evidence may also mean statements conveying sound medical principles found in medical treatises. It would also include statements contained in authoritative writings such as medical and scientific articles and research reports or analyses.*

It would be foolish to create a reductionistic and artificial distinction between "physiological" and "psychological" phenomena, particularly if it meant arguing that psychological issues can't impact the body. Anyone who has ever experienced a panic attack will tell you that mental health issues can certainly have a physical impact on the body, including breathing, and the chronic issues associated with PTSD can certainly, demonstrably have a multisystemic impact on health. Arguments that focus on the discipline of the reviewer or the fact that PTSD is "psychological" rather than "physiological" are fallacious and attempt to avoid addressing the significant interactions that exist between the two. In this instance the relevant questions do not just include where sleep apnea comes from, but what impact PTSD has on the development and progression of sleep apnea.

SHOULD VA EXAMINERS BE GIVEN MORE WEIGHT THAN PRIVATE DOCTORS?

No. According to the VA's own policies, evidence from VA and contract examiners should not automatically be given more weight than the evidence from private professionals. The VA's policies note *"when evaluating medical and lay evidence from non-VA sources accept it at face value unless there is reason to question its competency or credibility. Non-VA evidence does not have inherently less probative value than evidence originated by VA. Both VA and non-VA evidence are objectively weighed in determinations of competency, credibility, and probative value."*

See the VA's "Standards of Evidentiary Proof" https://www.knowva.ebenefits.va.gov/system/templates/selfservice/va_ssnew/help/customer/locale/en-US/portal/554400000001018/content/554400000014383/M21-1,-Part-V,-Subpart-ii,-Chapter-1,-Section-A---Principles-of-Reviewing-and-Weighing-Evidence#1b)

WHAT IS THE VETERAN'S BURDEN OF PROOF ON VA DISABILITY CLAIMS?

The VA's "Standards of Evidentiary Proof" help us to understand what the burden of proof is on a VA disability claim (as opposed to other legal situations).

Every substantive or procedural factual matter must have a standard of proof whether stated explicitly or not. Standard of proof specifies the degree of persuasion or confidence in the evidence with regard to the subject of the proof that is required in order to find a fact proven.

Note: The application of standard of proof is qualitative, not quantitative. The question is weight or persuasiveness of the evidence and not the number of items of evidence. Evidence is not necessarily in relative equipoise when the number of acceptable items of evidence tending to support a fact is equal to the number of items tending to not support a fact.

The table below describes the different standards of evidentiary proof (relative equipoise is needed for VA disability cases):

Standard	Description
relative equipoise	Evidence must persuade the decision maker that the fact is as likely as not.
preponderance of the evidence	The greater weight of evidence is that the fact exists. The fact is more likely than not.
affirmative evidence to the contrary	The fact is unlikely; and the evidence against the matter is of greater weight. This standard is the opposite of the preponderance standard.
clear and convincing	The fact finder has reasonable certainty of the truth of a fact. This is a higher standard of proof than having to find a fact is more likely than not.
clear and unmistakable	The evidence must establish the fact without question.

As noted by the VA:

The reasonable doubt rule means that the evidence provided by the claimant/beneficiary (or obtained on the claimant's/beneficiary's behalf) must only persuade the decision maker that each factual matter is at least as likely as not.

It is the defined and consistently applied policy of the VA to administer the law under a broad interpretation, consistent, however, with the facts shown in every case. When, after careful consideration of all procurable and assembled data, a reasonable doubt arises regarding service origin, the degree of disability, or any other point, such doubt will be resolved in favor of the claimant.

In Gilbert v. Derwinski, 1 Vet.App. 49 (1990), CAVC noted that an equipoise decision is
necessarily more qualitative than quantitative; it is one not capable of mathematical precision and certitude. Equal weight is not accorded to each piece of material contained in the record; every item of evidence does not have the same probative value.

CAVC further likened the reasonable doubt rule as akin to the principle in baseball that the "tie goes to the runner."

Overwhelming imbalance? The VA notes "if the evidence shows an overwhelming imbalance, then the evidence requires a decision in that direction, either for or against awarding the claim. Note: The claim must be awarded if all of the evidence is favorable."

Reasonable doubt? The VA notes "as indicated at M21-1, Part V, Subpart ii, 1.A.1.j, resolve reasonable doubt in favor of the claimant if all procurable evidence, after being weighed, is found in approximate balance or equipoise. 38 CFR 3.102 dictates that the Veteran prevails when the evidence neither satisfactorily proves nor disproves an issue."

Raters should not be adversarial: The VA notes: "an adversarial system involves advocates representing contrary positions before an impartial decision maker. The VA system is non-adversarial. There is no advocate on behalf of VA opposing claims and no policy to minimize or deny benefits. Decision makers are expected to be impartial and liberally apply VA's pro-Veteran policies, procedures, and regulations in accordance with any applicable VA guidance. VA's policy is to award benefits where supported under the facts and law or when the evidence is in relative equipoise or balance while denying only when we must under the facts and law require it." The VA advises raters/ decision makers that:

Decision makers must
- *be objective and fair in the consideration of evidence*
- *ensure that any inferences, findings, and conclusions made are supported under the facts and law*
- *follow the evidentiary guidance in this chapter*
- *be professional and courteous even when claimants are antagonistic, critical, or abusive*
- *not allow any bias or personal feelings into the evaluation of evidence or the decision*
- *not arbitrarily or capriciously refuse to assign weight to a claimant's evidence, and*
- *not adopt or express an adversarial position towards a claimant or beneficiary.*

Important:
- *Do not refer to the claimant or beneficiary as a liar. Where evidence is not credible, say that and cite facts of record in support.*
- *Do not minimize the weight of a treating physician's opinion based upon the idea that the*

physician has become an advocate for the patient
since doing so may appear adversarial and biased.

It is notable that a VA disability case is different from some other things that a medical professional may be asked to comment on, and different from other types of legal cases. The burden of proof on a Veteran's disability case is at least as likely as not. That is, essentially, a 50/50 chance or 50/50 possibility like a coin flip. A 50% chance is not "just within the realm of possibility," but it is also not as high a burden as whatever "medical certainty" or "psychological certainty" tends to imply. It is not 95% probability nor is it any of the other tests for different types of legal cases. Sometimes professionals use phrases like "psychological certainty" or "medical certainty," though I'm certain they have no idea what those phrases even imply. At least as likely as not, sometimes phrased as at least in equipoise, implies an opinion that one side is at least as likely as another. This is not a quantitative opinion but a qualitative one, though, as there is rarely the ability to mathematically establish exact percentages of this nature scientifically. As noted earlier, "38 CFR 3.102 dictates that the Veteran prevails when the evidence neither satisfactorily proves nor disproves an issue."

When Veterans' claims for sleep apnea secondary to PTSD are denied, it often centers around different interpretations of whether or not the connection itself is at least as likely as not. In instances where the Veteran has a sleep apnea diagnosis established and a PTSD service connection already established, the denial rarely has anything to do with something specific about the Veteran's own medical history and evidence, the denial has to do with the way an examiner and/or rater chose to interpret the science and the burden of proof on that Veteran's case. The "qualitative" and subjective piece to that determination.

Based on some informal research I conducted which is described later in this book, you'll see that it's also at least as likely as not that those denials will later on get overturned when a Veteran's claim goes to BVA. With BVA there is a high chance (potentially a 50/50 chance) that the previous denial for sleep apnea secondary to PTSD will be overturned and the Veteran will be granted for sleep apnea secondary to PTSD.

Based on the data, there is a high likelihood that denials for sleep apnea secondary to PTSD will be overturned and approved. The high likelihood that denials for sleep apnea secondary to PTSD will be overturned and approved reflects problems with the VA system, given that if a Veteran's claim is going to be approved it should be done at the earliest and least expensive point possible. This is particularly relevant when you consider that the only difference on many denials and approvals is that the VA's examiner (and in response the VA's decision maker) interprets the science in a way that keeps them from concluding that the evidence neither satisfactorily proves nor disproves the issue- at least as likely as not. On some Veterans' claims, the VA says that the science is at least in equipoise for sleep apnea secondary to PTSD, whereas on other Veterans' claims the VA concludes that the science isn't at least in equipoise. The denial is centered around the science and the examiner's interpretation of the science, not something from the Veteran's own medical evidence. The approvals and denials are based on the VA's own internally inconsistent interpretation of the science. It is off putting that on the same day the VA can say that the scientific evidence is at least in equipoise for one veteran, but then say that the science says the opposite for a different veteran. Many times these conclusions are just based on the opinions of a specific C&P examiner, who may or may not have any substantial expertise in sleep apnea or PTSD.

WHY NOT JUST GET A NEXUS LETTER FROM YOUR TREATMENT PROVIDER RATHER THAN PAY FOR A NEXUS LETTER FROM A FORENSIC PROFESSIONAL?

Sometimes a Veteran's treatment provider is willing to write a nexus letter, but this can be the exception rather than the rule due to ethical reasons (particularly on the part of mental health providers). If a treatment provider is willing and able-- they have sufficient expertise to do it correctly without inadvertently creating problems —then there is no reason for a Veteran to decline the help. When a treatment provider does offer a nexus opinion, that can be very helpful for the Veteran as they won't have to go through the trouble of working with a provider who has not yet met them or reviewed their records or pay the additional cost to that private professional (though treatment providers may charge for opinions as well). Sometimes treatment providers charge for this service and sometimes they do not. Raters from administrative bodies like the VA on paper often indicate that they favor opinions from treatment providers (even though this technically is not their policy), however, in practice it often seems like they are apt to go with the opinion of a C&P examiner even though the treatment provider often has a longer relationship with the Veteran.

The VA is on alert for fraud in relation to private providers who Veterans don't have an ongoing treatment relationship with. Prior to the pandemic, the VA's Office of Inspector General wrote reports noting that telehealth public use questionnaires were used improperly to determine disability benefits. These reports were written prior to a VA policy change during the pandemic that allowed telehealth visits from private professionals and is now primarily moot in that respect. In the report "the OIG underscored the need for VBA to implement adequate controls on the use of publicly available [DBQ] forms, whose content could be altered to support baseless or exaggerated disability claims." They wrote "at issue were healthcare providers who did not practice in the state, territory, or county where the veterans reside allegedly being paid to complete the public-use questionnaires and document conditions meriting disability benefits without ever seeing the veteran in person." The OIG noted that these questionnaires were being completed via "telehealth" and in the report had to define telehealth (though at this point following the pandemic we all know what telehealth is, though at that time the "use of private provider telehealth examinations for rating purposes is prohibited"). As you can see there are old attitudes where simply being in another "county" from the provider could lead to a suspicion of fraud. However, in many areas of the country Veterans have to go to another county to get to a VA, let alone a specialized treatment provider. This is an unfortunate attitude related to different locations/counties given that a 2015 analysis by the American Psychological Association found that "approximately 34.5 percent of the counties in the nation" had no record of a licensed psychologist even living there. That is more than one third of the counties in the nation. 66.4% of counties in the United States had no more than 5 psychologists and 74.6% of counties had no more than 10 psychologists. A link to those findings:

https://www.apa.org/workforce/publications/15-county-analysis#:~:text=Approximately %2034.5%20percent%20of%20the%20counties%20in %20the,of%20counties%20had%20no%20more %20than%20ten%20psychologists.

Now consider that only a limited number of professionals are familiar with forensically evaluating impairment adequately under any system, let alone the VA's system. In a world where a high percentage of counties have no psychologist at all, it makes sense that Veterans would use evolving telehealth technology and evolving legal structures like The Psychology Interjurisdictional Compact (PSYPACT) to legally speak with psychologists (or other professionals) who have the specialized expertise that they need.

The concerns about telehealth were not empirically

justified. The VA shouldn't be able to realistically complain about telehealth exams themselves given that two of its own employees performed a study and concluded that there was no difference in quality between telehealth and in person C&P examinations [*See Gianoli, M. O., & Meisler, A. W. (2022). PTSD disability examinations in the Department of Veterans Affairs: A comparison of telehealth and in-person exams. Professional Psychology: Research and Practice.* https://psycnet.apa.org/doiLanding?doi=10.1037%2Fpro0000479].

Gisnoli & Meisler (2022) noted *"it is estimated that the VA will have rendered decisions on roughly 1.4 million disability claims in 2021. A substantial percentage of these are for mental health conditions, specifically posttraumatic stress disorder (PTSD). Prior to the COVID-19 pandemic, almost all Compensation and Pension (C&P) examinations for PTSD were completed in-person; since March 2020, most have been conducted using telehealth."* They noted that *"the present study compared Initial PTSD examinations by telehealth to those completed in-person. Overall, 105 reports (51 in-person and 54 telehealth) were randomly selected from all Initial PTSD C&P exams completed within VA Connecticut between 2019 and 2020 (1 year preceding the pandemic and the first year of the pandemic). Raters were masked to all information indicating examiner, mode, and date of exam. Exam content was recorded, and exam quality was rated using three metrics that demonstrated adequate reliability and sensitivity in a prior study. There were no statistically significant differences between in-person and tele-exams on any relevant report content variables, report quality metrics, or VA disability rating outcomes. Results support the validity of the use of telehealth for conducting psychological exams for PTSD disability claims within the VA."*

The VA's now defunct prohibition related to private telehealth DBQ's appears even more absurd in the context of changes following the pandemic. More and more mental health providers are providing telehealth by default. In addition, more and more are increasingly practicing across state borders and marketing niche practice specialties that Veterans and others in rural areas previously had no access to (particularly since there wasn't even a single psychologist in their county). Before this their choice was either to travel a considerable distance or go without help. Now, professional compacts exist that allow professionals licensed in one state to practice to many other states via telehealth. For example, psychologists approved through PSYPACT can legally offer telehealth services to more than half the states (and the list keeps growing). For a current list related to psychologists you can follow this link:

https://psypact.site-ym.com/general/custom.asp?page=psypactmap

This has opened up the opportunity for Veterans to have easier access to forensic specialists who were often previously only available to Veterans living in big cities. It would be an error for the VA to simply dismiss and disregard these expert opinions simply because the Veteran lived in a different location, such as a rural, underserved area. Before considering locations, other signs of fraud should be present, and the weight and credibility of an opinion should be determined by the facts and the strength of the opinion itself (not just whether or not someone was in a different location). It is not simply "doctor-shopping" if a Veterans wants to speak with an experienced specialist that they can't find in their own area.

Veterans have an important right to seek their own second opinions and independent medical opinions from their own experts, and there is no evidence based reason they should not be able to do this via telehealth as well. This is particularly relevant given that the VA's own Office of Inspector General issued a 6/8/2022 report titled *"Contract Medical Exam Program Limitations Put Veterans at Risk for Inaccurate Claims Decisions."* The VA's own OIG notes that the exams the VA purchases can be of low quality. Per the VA's OIG "contract exams are a significant investment, and VA has spent nearly $6.8 billion since fiscal year 2017. Some of the exams produced by vendors have not met contractual accuracy requirements. As a result, claims processors may have used inaccurate or insufficient medical evidence to decide veterans' claims. Therefore, it is vital for VBA to improve the governance and accountability of the program." The OIG found that the contractors QTC, VES and LHI "failed to consistently provide VBA with the accurate exams required by the contracts." The OIG notes that "ALL THREE VENDORS HAVE BEEN BELOW THE CONTRACT'S 92% ACCURACY REQUIREMENT SINCE AT LEAST 2017." Most errors– including a significant number that "had the potential to affect claims decisions–" aren't corrected before the claims processors decided the claims per the OIG. We know that the VA's own OIG has found that the contract exams that the VA pays for do not live up to the quality standards that the VA has set for them. They have consistently failed to meet their quality targets. If Veterans are in a situation where an inaccurate, incomplete or otherwise flawed C&P examination is impacting their claim, they often have few options other than to look for second opinions. It is disingenuous for the VA to suggest that the cure for a problem is more of the problem (ex: inaccurate C&P exams). While we do have to watch out for certain professionals who may be acting in an unethical manner, that doesn't mean that all, or even most forensic professionals are acting in an unethical manner. In reality, some C&P examiners hired by the VA and/or one of the VA's contractors may also be at risk for acting in an unethical manner (particularly when the pay for the VA contractors is very low compared to the private sector and there is an incentive for them to churn out DBQ's quickly in a "volume" business). These concerns are consistent with a published article by VA employees (VA Connecticut Healthcare System). They criticize the quality of VA contract exams [see: Meisler, A. W., & Gianoli, M. O. (2022). The Department of Veterans Affairs disability examination program for PTSD: Critical analysis and strategies for remediation. Psychology, Public Policy, and Law].

The authors take exams from VA contractors (i.e. QTC, VES, LHI) to task noting *"there are several possible explanations for the observed deficiencies in contract exams, including lack of supervision, more limited access to VA treatment records, and inadequate training and experience. An additional explanation is that, unlike exams by salaried VA staff, contractors are paid a flat fee for each exam which is a small fraction of the typical fees paid for forensic psychological evaluation in the community. Thus, there is a financial incentive to complete exams quickly, which would preclude careful record review, psychological testing, and detailed report preparation."*

Interestingly, while suggesting that the "flat fee" which is a "small fraction of the typical fees paid for forensic psychological evaluation in the community..." is a problem, the authors did not propose solutions to this such as increasing the fees paid for the exams in order to attract better educated and more experienced forensic experts to the work or address issues with the contract exams being a volume business where examiners have to churn out a number of exams in order to keep the lights on due to the low pay from VES, QTC and LHI. Highly experienced forensic professionals who could offer ethical, high quality exams do not gravitate to or stay in the work long given that, as the authors note, the VA contractors pay a "small fraction of the typical fees paid" in the community. The article authors go on to suggest that *"anecdotally, it is not uncommon for veterans seen by contractors needing to be reexamined, at times with requests for second and even third opinions to resolve "conflicting medical evidence" after a contract examiner rendered an opinion that contradicted those in the veteran's records or in previous C&P exams. Inefficiencies resulting from poor exams increase the workload for both examiners and VBA personnel and increase the costs for VA C&P operations overall."* The authors also note *"although raters are not expected to become experts in psychology, they are tasked with making critical determinations about cases in which complex issues of psychological causation and apportionment are central, subject matter in which they likely have little or no knowledge or training."*

Given that the VA may try to view private opinions

obtained by the Veteran skeptically and given that the quality of the exam paid for by the VA can be a roll-of-the-dice, it would make sense for the Veteran to try to get an opinion from their own treatment provider, right? The VA's private mental health related DBQ's even have a spot where it asks if the Veteran is regularly seen by them (i.e. in treatment). The publicly available DBQ's note that they are "intended" for use by their provider. However, anecdotally, the VA in practice may discount the opinions of treatment providers and obtain their own C&P examination, then favor that opinion (despite the fact that statistically we know that that exam may not be of a higher quality than an exam performed by a better-paid forensic expert in the community and despite the fact that a C&P examiner often knows less about the Veteran than a treatment provider). We also know that a contradictory recommendation in policy exists, at least for mental health professionals, which decreases the likelihood that treatment providers will offer an opinion.

VA policy also offers a professional ethics-based head-fake to Veterans which limits their ability to get mental health related nexus letters from VA treatment providers. While it would be convenient if Veterans in need of first or second opinions on mental health related claims could seek them from treatment providers at the VA, VA policy outlined in *VHA Directive 1134(2) Provision of Medical Statements and Completion of Forms by VA Health Care Providers* recommends that VA mental health treatment providers not complete forms such as "mental health DBQ's" in order to "maintain the integrity of the patient-provider relationship." Therefore, both the VA and Veterans often must seek forensic specialists outside of a treatment relationship to provide opinions related to their case. The VA's own policy and the professional ethics of mental health providers discourages treatment providers from providing these opinions for Veterans.

See https://www.va.gov/vhapublications/ViewPublication.asp?pub_ID=4300

While the VA raters might be skeptical of the higher quality forensic professionals from the community when they see the button on the DBQ checked that the person was not the Veteran's treatment provider, the reality is both VA policy and professional ethics suggest that this is the best arrangement to "maintain the integrity" of the treatment relationship. Derisive epithets such as "doctor shopping" are therefore undeserved, as this is the most ethical arrangement based on VA policy and professional ethics. Ethical forensic professionals provide independent opinions, not rubber stamps. The ethics of the profession attempts to keep treatment services and forensic services separate and distinct. This is why the VA's own policy discourages VA mental health treatment providers from actually completing nexus letters or DBQ forms. Our professional ethics suggests that the treatment provider and the independent professional giving an unbiased look should be different people. In a system which is not supposed to be adversarial but where the VA's own OIG indicates that the opinion that the VA pays for from a contract examiner can be of low quality (and where those same C&P exams can read as adversarial), it is reasonable that Veterans will sometimes wish to seek their own independent expert opinions. The VA can hire its expert. The veteran can hire their own expert as well.

ETHICS AND FORENSIC PROFESSIONALS

When a treatment provider is unable or unwilling to offer disability-related opinions, Veterans can go to an independent forensic professional to be evaluated (either via an examination with a medical records review or a records review alone).

Dr. Finnerty is a forensic specialist and adheres to the *American Psychological Association's Ethical Principles of Psychologists and Code of Conduct* as well as the APA's *Specialty Guidelines for Forensic Psychology* (https://www.apa.org/practice/guidelines/forensic-psychology). These guidelines include the responsibilities of integrity, impartiality and fairness and note: *"When offering expert opinions to be relied upon by a decision maker, providing forensic therapeutic services, or teaching or conducting research, forensic practitioners strive for accuracy, impartiality, fairness, and independence. Forensic practitioners recognize the adversarial nature of the legal system and strive to treat all participants and weigh all data, opinions, and rival hypotheses impartially. When conducting forensic examinations, forensic practitioners strive to be unbiased and impartial, and avoid partisan presentation of unrepresentative, incomplete, or inaccurate evidence that might mislead finders of fact. This guideline does not preclude forceful presentation of the data and reasoning upon which a conclusion or professional product is based."*

At times VA raters have suggested in their rating decision narratives that they write that a professional who isn't a C&P examiner and isn't a "treatment provider" is automatically "biased" in favor of the Veteran who paid them for an independent opinion. While it may help the rater unfairly and fallaciously disregard evidence in favor of the Veteran that they don't want to address, this, of course, is not how our professional ethics work. The rater is essentially accusing the licensed professional of unethical behavior. We know that treatment providers often defer to forensic providers to avoid multiple roles and the tendency to want to advocate for their patient. Who are they deferring to? They are deferring to specialized forensic professionals like Dr. Finnerty.

The APA's Specialty Guidelines for Forensic Psychology outline how this should work. You can see the entire document here: https://www.apa.org/practice/guidelines/forensic-psychology

Here are some relevant excerpts that raters concerned about bias should be familiar with. Forensic professionals must strive to provide independent and unbiased opinions.

1.01 Integrity
Forensic practitioners strive for accuracy, honesty, and truthfulness in the science, teaching, and practice of forensic psychology and they strive to resist partisan pressures

to provide services in any ways that might tend to be misleading or inaccurate.

1.02 Impartiality and Fairness
When offering expert opinion to be relied upon by a decision maker, providing forensic therapeutic services, or teaching or conducting research, forensic practitioners strive for accuracy, impartiality, fairness, and independence (EPPCC Standard 2.01). Forensic practitioners recognize the adversarial nature of the legal system and strive to treat all participants and weigh all data, opinions, and rival hypotheses impartially.

When conducting forensic examinations, forensic practitioners strive to be unbiased and impartial, and avoid partisan presentation of unrepresentative, incomplete, or inaccurate evidence that might mislead finders of fact. This guideline does not preclude forceful presentation of the data and reasoning upon which a conclusion or professional product is based.

When providing educational services, forensic practitioners seek to represent alternative perspectives, including data, studies, or evidence on both sides of the question, in an accurate, fair and professional manner, and strive to weigh and present all views, facts, or opinions impartially.

When conducting research, forensic practitioners seek to represent results in a fair and impartial manner. Forensic practitioners strive to utilize research designs and scientific methods that adequately and fairly test the questions at hand, and they attempt to resist partisan pressures to develop designs or report results in ways that might be misleading or unfairly bias the results of a test, study, or evaluation.

1.03 Avoiding Conflicts of Interest
Forensic practitioners refrain from taking on a professional role when personal, scientific, professional, legal, financial, or other interests or relationships could reasonably be expected to impair their impartiality, competence, or effectiveness, or expose others with whom a professional relationship exists to harm (EPPCC Standard 3.06).

Forensic practitioners are encouraged to identify, make known, and address real or apparent conflicts of interest in an attempt to maintain the public confidence and trust, discharge professional obligations, and maintain responsibility, impartiality, and accountability (EPPCC Standard 3.06). Whenever possible, such conflicts are revealed to all parties as soon as they become known to the psychologist. Forensic practitioners consider whether a prudent and competent forensic practitioner engaged in similar circumstances would determine that the ability to make a proper decision is likely to become impaired under the immediate circumstances.

When a conflict of interest is determined to be manageable, continuing services are provided and documented in a way to manage the conflict, maintain accountability, and preserve the trust of relevant others (also see Section 4.02 below).

We know that professionals should not typically provide both forensic opinions (example, opinions related to disability) and treatment services. Some of the references from the profession's ethical guidelines are:

4.02 Multiple Relationships
A multiple relationship occurs when a forensic practitioner

is in a professional role with a person and, at the same time or at a subsequent time, is in a different role with the same person; is involved in a personal, fiscal, or other relationship with an adverse party; at the same time is in a relationship with a person closely associated with or related to the person with whom the forensic practitioner has the professional relationship; or offers or agrees to enter into another relationship in the future with the person or a person closely associated with or related to the person (EPPCC Standard 3.05).

Forensic practitioners strive to recognize the potential conflicts of interest and threats to objectivity inherent in multiple relationships. Forensic practitioners are encouraged to recognize that some personal and professional relationships may interfere with their ability to practice in a competent and impartial manner and they seek to minimize any detrimental effects by avoiding involvement in such matters whenever feasible or limiting their assistance in a manner that is consistent with professional obligations.

4.02.01 Therapeutic-Forensic Role Conflicts

Providing forensic and therapeutic psychological services to the same individual or closely related individuals involves multiple relationships that may impair objectivity and/or cause exploitation or other harm. Therefore, when requested or ordered to provide either concurrent or sequential forensic and therapeutic services, forensic practitioners are encouraged to disclose the potential risk and make reasonable efforts to refer the request to another qualified provider. If referral is not possible, the forensic practitioner is encouraged to consider the risks and benefits to all parties and to the legal system or entity likely to be impacted, the possibility of separating each service widely in time, seeking judicial review and direction, and consulting with knowledgeable colleagues. When providing both forensic and therapeutic services, forensic practitioners seek to minimize the potential negative effects of this circumstance (EPPCC Standard 3.05).

CONTINGENT FEES ARE TYPICALLY NOT ETHICAL FOR EXPERTS

A contingent fee is a fee based on a percentage of what someone may "win" in a claim. Physicians and psychologists are not able to charge in this manner as it is not ethical for them to. Both the American Medical Association and the American Psychological Association have come out against physicians and psychologists charging "contingent" fees. This type of fee is relatively common for attorneys, as attorneys are expected to be partisan. However, health care professionals you hire for your claim are not expected to be partisan or an advocate for you- they are an advocate for the facts of a case. They are an expert witness; their opinions should not be viewed as unduly influenced or purchased by the highest bidder. Attorneys also have strict rules on what and how they can charge (ex: see https://www.vetadvocates.org/cpages/fees-which-may-be-charged-by-agent-attorney).

I'd be careful of any doctor that wants to take a percentage of your VA claim pay; they may not be acting ethically or consistent with the strict rules that attorneys have to work under. Some organizations which try to charge this way are neither a doctor or an attorney or VA accredited representative. They may be paying a fixed fee to a doctor and then charging you more. If you just need a nexus letter or DBQ exam (rather than the other claim consultation services these organizations sometimes indicate they offer) there are doctors out there willing to work with you directly in an ethical manner with fixed fees for their time that you are aware of up front without any surprise billing (surprise billing is also not ethical and could be illegal depending on the circumstances).

SLEEP APNEA SECONDARY TO PTSD

Based on the DSM-5-TR, posttraumatic stress disorder (PTSD) is the development of characteristic symptoms following exposure to one or more traumatic events. The clinical presentation of PTSD "varies." The DSM-5-TR (pg. 311) notes that PTSD is associated with high impairment in social, occupational and physical functioning; reduced quality of life; "and physical health problems." The American Psychiatric Association's diagnostic manual for PTSD literally indicates that PTSD is associated with "physical health problems."

Per the NIH, "sleep apnea is a common condition in which your breathing stops and restarts many times while you sleep. This can prevent your body from getting enough oxygen. You may want to talk to your healthcare provider about sleep apnea if someone tells you that you snore or gasp during sleep, or if you experience other symptoms of poor-quality sleep, such as excessive daytime sleepiness." The NIH notes "obstructive sleep apnea happens when your upper airway becomes blocked many times while you sleep, reducing or completely stopping airflow. This is the most common type of sleep apnea. Anything that could narrow your airway such as obesity, large tonsils, or changes in your hormone levels can increase your risk for obstructive sleep apnea." They note "central sleep apnea happens when your brain does not send the signals needed to breathe. Health conditions that affect how your brain controls your airway and chest muscles can cause central sleep apnea" [see https://www.nhlbi.nih.gov/health/sleep-apnea].

Is there a relationship between sleep apnea and PTSD? The VA's own website appears to indicate a "relationship." While some C&P examiners note they aren't "related," it is notable that the VA's own website implies a "relationship" between sleep apnea and PTSD and cites a study from Colvonen, et. al. for support (see the VA's website at https://www.research.va.gov/topics/respiratory.cfm).

The VA's own website notes *"Sleep apnea (pauses in breathing that occur at night) can cause excessive daytime sleepiness, trouble concentrating, high blood pressure, cardiac and pulmonary disease, and motor vehicle accidents.*

Relationship with PTSD—In 2016, researchers at the VA San Diego Healthcare System and the University of California found that the risk of obstructive sleep apnea among Iraq and Afghanistan Veterans increased with the severity of their PTSD symptoms.

The investigators looked at 195 Iraq and Afghanistan Veterans—more than 93% were men—who had visited a VA outpatient PTSD clinic for evaluation of their symptoms. Using clinical questionnaires to evaluate both levels of PTSD and sleep apnea risk, researchers found that nearly 70% of Veterans in the study were at high risk for developing sleep apnea, and that the risk increased with the severity of their

PTSD symptoms. This was despite the fact that many of them did not have a high body mass index or high blood pressure, considered risk factors for sleep apnea."

The VA's own website supports the existence of a "relationship" and that PTSD is a significant risk factor for sleep apnea. This is interesting given that it is common for some VA C&P examiners to simply state that there is "no relationship" between sleep apnea and PTSD without citing any relevant evidence supporting this. However, any opinion that suggests that there is no relationship at all between the two is incorrect and both inconsistent with the science and inconsistent with the VA's own website. These examiner's opinions should be disregarded as inadequate given their rationale which is not adequately supported and inconsistent with the VA's own website. It is also not adequate for a C&P examiner to simply say "PTSD does not cause sleep apnea." This not only fails to address substantial aggravation, it fails to adequately address the potential processes by which PTSD may at least as likely as not lead to and worsen sleep apnea.

When it comes to forensic rationales, "because I say so" or fallaciously appealing to authority by saying "because I'm the doctor" is never sufficient and adequate. It also isn't adequate to overgeneralize and mischaracterize what "studies show" or do not show without citing the actual evidence. This shouldn't be acceptable or adequate for any professional on either side, despite the rationales of many C&P examinations simply saying "there is no relationship" or "there is no evidence" when this is in fact not an accurate representation even based on the VA's own website. When a Veteran contends that it is at least as at least as likely as not that their sleep apnea is secondary to their PTSD, then the rationale and reasoning used by VA examiners to address this should at least be adequate. Likewise, a nexus letter needs to offer adequate support as to why it is at least as likely as not that the Veteran's sleep apnea is secondary to their PTSD.

CONTROVERSY IN RELATION TO SLEEP APNEA SECONDARY TO PTSD CLAIMS

There is some controversy when it comes to connecting sleep apnea secondary to PTSD; not all C&P examiners agree with making the connection. In relation to the science, not everything in relation to causality is necessarily 100% certain. With that being said, science does not operate on 100% certainty and neither do forensic opinions. In the context of VA disability claims, the Veteran's burden of proof is also not 100% certainty. Depending on the question, it isn't always even related to causality but substantial aggravation. For sleep apnea secondary to PTSD; it isn't always necessary that the PTSD cause sleep apnea. The controversy is easy to see when different VA C&P examiners will come down on different sides of whether or not the evidence meets the Veteran's burden of proof of at least as likely as not. It is easy to see when on the same day VA decisionmakers will find that the science says one thing for one Veteran but for another Veteran they will conclude that the science says something else.

There are common reasons why sleep apnea secondary

to PTSD claims are denied. First, Veterans need to have actually been diagnosed with sleep apnea and also need to establish a service connection for PTSD or another mental health concern for sleep apnea to be secondary to it. This seems overly basic but there are a number of denials for sleep apnea secondary to PTSD that are based on the fact that the Veteran was not diagnosed with sleep apnea yet (it appears that the Veteran filed hoping to have the VA send them to a sleep study to find out if they had sleep apnea but instead the VA simply denied their case instead of helping them find out if they had sleep apnea).

There are denials based on C&P examinations where the examiner focused on what sleep apnea is characterized by, not what the Veteran's own sleep apnea was caused by- they describe what sleep apnea is but don't address PTSD or mental health issues specifically (or the related evidence). The opinions focus on "causation" and fail to adequately address substantial aggravation. The analysis tends to reflect that the examiner used a burden of proof related to causation that was higher than at least as likely as not, reviewing scientific evidence in the Veteran's favor as not sufficient to meet their overly rigorous, subjective standard. Sometimes the examiners focus on the Veteran's weight, yet then do not address the evidence that a Veteran's weight could at least as likely as not be increased by mental health difficulties. Mental health difficulties like PTSD can impact eating behaviors and activity levels.

Some C&P examiners make vague generalities about what sleep apnea is, then fail to actually address anything from the Veteran's own specific medical evidence or address the actual scientific evidence related to sleep apnea secondary to PTSD. When it comes to the science, there's multiple ways that PTSD could at least as likely as not cause and/or substantially aggravate sleep apnea. As noted, one way is potentially through weight gain and obesity. It is amusing that examiners will indicate that PTSD only has an "association" or is a risk factor for sleep apnea, then in their argument recite a laundry list of other things that the Veteran's sleep apnea was likely due to which are also established as risk factors and/or only have evidence for an association. For example, being male does not cause sleep apnea, yet it is commonly referenced by some C&P examiners. Examiners will throw out a laundry list of things that are shown to be associated with sleep apnea or risk factors of sleep apnea after having just argued that there's only evidence for an association with sleep apnea when it comes to PTSD. While evidence of an association does not equal 100% evidence of causation, as noted the Veteran's burden of proof is not 100% certainty of causation. The examiner's tasks is to evaluate the full extent of the scientific and medical evidence and formulate an opinion related to what is at least as likely as not in the Veteran's specific case- not copy and paste an overly-generic, non-peer-reviewed text from UpToDate or a Google search.

A rationale that sometimes appears in denial rating decisions and C&P opinions is that "OSA is not a psychological disorder. It is a medical condition..." However, this is not a relevant argument- it is a fallacious straw man argument that does not disprove anything in the case. No one was suggesting that OSA is "psychological disorder." This fallacious argument ignores the fact that psychological issues can in fact have an impact on the physical body (anyone who has ever had a panic attack will certainly agree that mental health conditions can impact breathing and the physical body). Mental health conditions can impact and even cause physical conditions. Also, while sleep apnea is not a psychiatric disorder per se, it is relevant enough to psychiatry that the American Psychiatric Association included sleep apnea in the *Diagnostic and Statistical Manual of Mental Disorders* (DSM-5-TR); [for example, see pages 429-443].

Another common statement that appears in denial rating decisions and C&P examiner's opinions is that sleep apnea is "a separate entity entirely" from PTSD. Of course it is, yet this is also a fallacious argument that is irrelevant to the question. Of course they are separate entities-- of course they are different diagnoses that should be rated separately-- however that does not preclude one from causing or substantially aggravating the other. No one argued that they were the same entity; this is a fallacious straw man argument which fails to address the actual questions on the Veteran's claim. Sometimes rating decisions and examiners will state that PTSD is unrelated to sleep apnea, however, this is not evidenced based. Suggesting that they are not "medically related" is an inadequate opinion which fails to meet the requirements of VA's policies for medical opinions. It is also inconsistent with the VA's own website which indicates that they are related. It is notable that the VA's own website indicates that sleep apnea has a "relationship with PTSD" (see https://www.research.va.gov/topics/respiratory.cfm#research8).

It is fallacious for examiners to create a reductionistic and artificial distinction between "physiological" and "psychological" phenomena, particularly when they seem to ridiculously argue that psychological issues can't impact the body (an argument that is not evidence based). The chronic issues associated with PTSD can certainly, demonstrably have a multisystemic impact on health. The DSM-5-TR indicates PTSD is associated with "physical health problems." Arguments that focus on mental health conditions as only "psychological" rather than "physiological" are fallacious and attempt to avoid addressing the significant interactions that exist between the two. This type of fallacious argument ignores the fact that psychological issues can in fact have an impact on the physical body (and as noted, anyone who has ever had a panic attack will know mental health conditions can impact breathing).

WEIGHT GAIN, OBESITY AND SLEEP APNEA FROM A MENTAL HEALTH PERSPECTIVE

PTSD negatively impacts motivation (ex: reducing activity) and can lead to overeating and even binge eating. Subthreshold and threshold post-traumatic stress disorder (PTSD) are associated with binge eating symptoms in both men and women based on: [*Braun J, El-Gabalawy R, Sommer JL, Pietrzak RH, Mitchell K, Mota N. Trauma exposure, DSM-5 posttraumatic stress, and binge eating symptoms: results from a nationally representative sample. The Journal of Clinical Psychiatry. 2019;80(6):19m12813*]. Hoerster, et. al. (2015) noted in "PTSD and depression symptoms are associated with binge eating among US Iraq and Afghanistan veterans" [*see Eating Behaviors; Volume 17, April 2015, Pages 115-118*] that "PTSD and depression are common conditions among Iraq/Afghanistan Veterans. In the present study, PTSD and depression symptoms were associated with meeting binge eating screening criteria, identifying a possible pathway by which psychiatric conditions lead to disproportionate burden of overweight and obesity in this Veteran cohort." Doerflinger & Masheb (2018), in the research article "PTSD is associated with emotional eating among veterans seeking treatment for overweight/obesity" [*see Eating Behaviors, Volume 31, December 2018, Pages 8-11*] presented findings that "suggest that emotional eating is common among veterans reporting PTSD symptoms, and that any degree of PTSD symptom severity is associated with more frequent emotional eating."

Mental health difficulties can impact eating behaviors and activity levels essentially by definition. This can influence weight gain. For example, it is notable that major depressive disorder in the DSM-5-TR (pg. 183) lists diagnostic criteria such as "markedly diminished interest or pleasure in all, or almost all, activities most of the day, nearly every day..." and "significant weight loss when not dieting or weight gain (e.g., a change of more than 5% of body weight in a month), or decrease or increase in appetite nearly every day..." and "psychomotor agitation or retardation," and "fatigue or loss of energy nearly every day" and others. PTSD (pg. 302) includes criteria like "markedly diminished interest or participation in significant activities). Overeating and inactivity are symptoms of mental health difficulties which lead to weight gain and obesity.

ALCOHOL USE AND SLEEP APNEA

The scientific literature demonstrates that alcohol use can make sleep apnea worse. For example, a recent meta-analysis on the topic reviewed 1,266 studies and concluded "alcohol consumption is associated with worsening severity of snoring, altered sleep architecture, AHI, as well as lowest oxygen saturation among patients susceptible to snoring and obstructive sleep apnea" [see Burgos-Sanchez C, Jones NN, Avillion M, Gibson SJ, Patel JA, Neighbors J, Zaghi S, Camacho M. Impact of Alcohol Consumption on Snoring and Sleep Apnea: A Systematic Review and Meta-analysis. Otolaryngol Head Neck Surg. 2020 Dec;163(6):1078-1086]. The American Academy of Sleep Medicine has practice guidelines related to sleep apnea. The American Academy of Sleep Medicine's practice guidelines related to obstructive sleep apnea include, as a standard of care in the field, that there be "patient education" on the impact of "alcohol avoidance" on sleep apnea. The "avoidance of alcohol" is also included as one of the "behavioral strategies" in managing sleep apnea [for the practice guidelines see Adult Obstructive Sleep Apnea Task Force of the American Academy of Sleep Medicine (2009), Epstein LJ; Kristo D; Strollo PJ; Friedman N; Malhotra A; Patil SP; Ramar K; Rogers R; Schwab RJ; Weaver EM; Weinstein MD. Clinical guideline for the evaluation, management and long-term care of obstructive sleep apnea in adults. J Clin Sleep Med 2009;5(3):263–276 https://doi.org/10.5664/jcsm.27497]. This reflects a recognition that the alcohol use which is sometimes tied to a Veteran's PTSD can substantially aggravate the Veteran's sleep apnea directly (in addition to also leading to a history of excessive caloric intake in the form of alcohol impacting weight gain and/or obesity).

HYPERAROUSAL- A LOW THRESHOLD FOR AROUSAL

One area that should be considered by professionals addressing PTSD and sleep apnea claims is the research related to PTSD, sleep apnea and hyperarousal/ a low threshold for arousal. There is at least a likely as not an arousal-based mechanism initiated by PTSD that promotes the development of sleep apnea in trauma survivors. This is supported by the article Krakow, B., Melendrez, D., Warner, T.D. et al. To Breathe, Perchance to Sleep: Sleep-Disordered Breathing and Chronic Insomnia Among Trauma Survivors. Sleep Breath 6, 189–202 (2002): *Emerging evidence invites a broader comorbidity perspective, based on recent findings that post-traumatic sleep disturbance frequently manifests with the combination of insomnia and a higher-than-expected prevalence of sleep-disordered breathing (SDB). In this model of complex sleep disturbance, the underlying sleep pathophysiology interacts with PTSD and related psychiatric distress; and this relationship appears very important as demonstrated by improvement in insomnia, nightmares, and post-traumatic stress with successful SDB treatment, independent of psychiatric interventions. Continuous positive airway pressure treatment in PTSD patients with SDB reduced electroencephalographic arousals and sleep fragmentation, which are usually attributed to central nervous system or psychophysiological processes. Related findings and clinical experience suggest that other types of chronic insomnia may also be related to SDB. We hypothesize that an arousal-based mechanism, perhaps initiated by post-traumatic stress and/or chronic insomnia, may promote the development of SDB in a trauma survivor and perhaps other patients with chronic insomnia. We discuss potential neurohormonal pathways and neuroanatomical sites that may be involved in this proposed interaction between insomnia and SDB.* These neurobiological processes are further reviewed by Kelly, et. al. (2016) in the article Understanding Recent Insights in Sleep and Posttraumatic Stress Disorder from a Research Domain Criteria (RDoC) Framework (Curr Sleep Medicine Rep, 2016, 2:223–232). They note that PTSD is associated with sleep disturbances, including insomnia, nightmares, REM abnormalities and "sleep-disordered breathing" such as in sleep apnea. They note that "recent studies have expanded our knowledge of the neurobiology of trauma and sleep. In addition, intervention research has provided valuable information about how sleep treatments affect PTSD symptoms and how PTSD treatments affect sleep symptoms." Chronic activation of stress hormones (hypothalamo-pituitary adrenal axis activity) caused by PTSD is known to lead to a neural sensitization leading to upper airway dysfunction such as sleep apnea. [see van Liempt, et. al. (2013) Sympathetic activity and hypothalamo-pituitary-adrenal axis activity during sleep in post-traumatic stress disorder: A study assessing polysomnography with simultaneous blood sampling. Psychoneuroendocrinology, 38(1), 155-165; and Kritikou, et. al. (2016) Sleep apnoea and the hypothalamic-pituitary-adrenal axis in men and women: effects of continuous positive airway pressure. European Respiratory Journal, 47(2):531-540.] PTSD at least as likely as not can cause airway instability through this hyperarousal, leading to sleep apnea concerns.

A Sample Nexus Letter from Dr. Finnerty

This is a sample nexus letter for J. Veteran (obviously a fictitious name). It is not related to any specific Veteran. A good nexus letter should also include more references to specific things in your own medical records such as diagnostic findings. For example, if you had past C&P denials/rating decisions that were relevant the letter would tend to address any specific opinions from those exams. The letter would also appear with letterhead information about Dr. Finnerty. While the text itself is copyright Todd Finnerty, LLC; Dr. Finnerty does not object to providers using the information for their own research and paraphrasing the information in their own words to help more Veterans.

Psychological File Review

Veteran's name: J. Veteran; (DOB/SSN)
Report date: XX/XX/XXXX
Reviewer: Todd Finnerty, Psy.D.
Records Reviewed: I have reviewed all the records provided from the Veteran's claims file. No examination was conducted for this medical opinion; I have performed a thorough review of the Veteran's medical history.

Referral Questions: The Veteran is applying for service connection for sleep apnea secondary to PTSD.

Analysis: Mr. Veteran experiences PTSD from his military service, including associated chronic sleep impairment based on his treatment records. The diagnostic criteria for PTSD include two separate symptoms associated with PTSD reflecting recurrent and distressing dreams as well as sleep disturbance such as difficulty falling asleep or staying asleep or restless sleep. This differs from the symptoms and impairment associated with sleep apnea. Mr. Veteran is also diagnosed with sleep apnea based on his treatment records.

There is ample evidence of multiple risk factors which show an association with sleep apnea-- one of these factors— at least as likely as not on par with the others or with stronger association than the others is PTSD; we also know the direction of the relationship as by definition PTSD is caused by trauma and PTSD is not caused by sleep apnea. These associated factors (ex: weight gain) can significantly contribute to the development of sleep apnea and/or substantially aggravate sleep apnea. There is scientific evidence that PTSD can also at least as likely as not cause sleep apnea through multiple pathways. Some C&P examiners perform a cursory review of data related to sleep apnea using resources such as UpToDate; UpToDate does not reflect an adequate literature review related to the evidence associated with sleep apnea being secondary to PTSD. It is not peer-reviewed research literature, it is geared toward giving a basic overview of the characteristics of sleep apnea to non-experts, and it does not address the growing body of primary source journal articles that are specifically related to sleep apnea secondary to PTSD. Citing sources such as UpToDate—or no sources at all-- is a sure sign that the examiner lacks relevant expertise in the subject matter. Some C&P

examiners attempt to describe what sleep apnea is characterized by as if this is what it is ultimately caused by, however this confuses the signs and symptoms of the sleep apnea process for sleep apnea's cause; this is an error. Factors such as sleeping position, weight gain, dentition, and pharyngeal anatomy are symptoms of or may worsen the symptoms of the sleep apnea process but do not necessarily reflect the ultimate cause of sleep apnea. His PTSD has likely had a profound impact on the development and subsequent substantial aggravation of his sleep apnea. Pharyngeal anatomy explains only a minimal portion of the variability in measures like the Apnea-Hypopnea Index (AHI). We know it is not just an anatomical disease when surgery to alter anatomy is of minimal benefit to a large number of individuals with OSA. Individuals with OSA often likely have hyperarousal concerns– a low threshold for arousal– which is an underlying mechanism of obstructive sleep apnea. Individuals have difficulty activating the muscles and stabilizing breathing in a normal fashion. PTSD can lead to this hyperarousal. The supporting research is outlined below. It is at least as likely as not that the Veteran's sleep apnea is secondary to his PTSD.

The incidence of insomnia and obstructive sleep apnea (OSA) in service members is increasing. "Between 2005 and 2019, incidence rates of OSA and insomnia increased from 11 to 333 and 6 to 272 (per 10,000), respectively." The incidence rates have "markedly increased" since 2005 [see Moore, et. al. (2021), Incidence of Insomnia and Obstructive Sleep Apnea in Active Duty United States Military Service Members. Sleep, doi: 10.1093/sleep/zsab024]. However, the evidence for service connection is not based on incidence rates alone. Significant associated factors that reflect both a causal relationship and substantial aggravation have been identified in the research literature and they are consistent with his mental health records. His mental health symptoms, which appear to be a response to traumatic stress from the military, have likely created a significant and substantial progression and increased severity of his sleep apnea above and beyond the natural progression of the disease. His sleep apnea aggravates his PTSD symptoms and his PTSD symptoms have substantially aggravated his sleep apnea. The course of the Veteran's sleep apnea is not inconsistent with exacerbation tied to traumatic stress and other psychiatric conditions including depression. There is scientific evidence supporting a link between his psychiatric disorders and his sleep apnea. The research literature establishes that PTSD is commonly associated with sleep apnea and that there is an arousal-based mechanism initiated by PTSD that promotes the development of sleep apnea in trauma survivors. Sharafkhaneh, et. Al. (2005), in the article Association of Psychiatric Disorders and Sleep Apnea in a Large Cohort (SLEEP, Vol. 28, No. 11, 2005) found that sleep apnea is associated with a higher prevalence of psychiatric comorbid conditions in Veterans Health Administration beneficiaries, including PTSD. Compared with patients not diagnosed with sleep apnea, a significantly greater prevalence (P < .0001) was found for posttraumatic stress disorder in patients with sleep apnea. The research supports the presence of a significant connection between PTSD and sleep apnea, including an arousal-based mechanism initiated by PTSD that promotes the development of sleep apnea in trauma survivors: This is supported by the article Krakow, B., Melendrez, D., Warner,

T.D. et al. To Breathe, Perchance to Sleep: Sleep-Disordered Breathing and Chronic Insomnia Among Trauma Survivors. Sleep Breath 6, 189–202 (2002): Emerging evidence invites a broader comorbidity perspective, based on recent findings that post-traumatic sleep disturbance frequently manifests with the combination of insomnia and a higher-than-expected prevalence of sleep-disordered breathing (SDB). In this model of complex sleep disturbance, the underlying sleep pathophysiology interacts with PTSD and related psychiatric distress; and this relationship appears very important as demonstrated by improvement in insomnia, nightmares, and post-traumatic stress with successful SDB treatment, independent of psychiatric interventions. Continuous positive airway pressure treatment in PTSD patients with SDB reduced electroencephalographic arousals and sleep fragmentation, which are usually attributed to central nervous system or psychophysiological processes. Related findings and clinical experience suggest that other types of chronic insomnia may also be related to SDB. We hypothesize that an arousal-based mechanism, perhaps initiated by post-traumatic stress and/or chronic insomnia, may promote the development of SDB in a trauma survivor and perhaps other patients with chronic insomnia. We discuss potential neurohormonal pathways and neuroanatomical sites that may be involved in this proposed interaction between insomnia and SDB. These neurobiological processes are further reviewed by Kelly, et. al. (2016) in the article Understanding Recent Insights in Sleep and Posttraumatic Stress Disorder from a Research Domain Criteria (RDoC) Framework (Curr Sleep Medicine Rep, 2016, 2:223–232). They note that PTSD is associated with sleep disturbances, including insomnia, nightmares,

REM abnormalities and "sleep-disordered breathing" such as in sleep apnea. They note that "recent studies have expanded our knowledge of the neurobiology of trauma and sleep. In addition, intervention research has provided valuable information about how sleep treatments affect PTSD symptoms and how PTSD treatments affect sleep symptoms." Chronic activation of stress hormones (hypothalamo-pituitary adrenal axis activity) caused by PTSD is known to lead to a neural sensitization leading to upper airway dysfunction such as sleep apnea. [see van Liempt, et. al. (2013) Sympathetic activity and hypothalamo-pituitary-adrenal axis activity during sleep in post-traumatic stress disorder: A study assessing polysomnography with simultaneous blood sampling. Psychoneuroendocrinology, 38(1), 155-165; and Kritikou, et. al. (2016) Sleep apnoea and the hypothalamic-pituitary-adrenal axis in men and women: effects of continuous positive airway pressure. European Respiratory Journal, 47(2):531-540.] PTSD causes airway instability through this hyperarousal, leading to sleep apnea concerns. Colvonen, et. al. (2015) [see Obstructive Sleep Apnea and Posttraumatic Stress Disorder among OEF/OIF/OND Veterans; Journal of Clinical Sleep Medicine 11(5):513-518] found that "PTSD symptom severity increased the risk of screening positive for OSA." The authors concluded that "veterans with PTSD screen as high risk for OSA at much higher rates..." Zhang, et. al. (2017) [see Prevalence of obstructive sleep apnea in patients with posttraumatic stress disorder and its impact on adherence to continuous positive airway pressure therapy: a meta analysis; Sleep Medicine, 36:125-132] performed a metal-analysis and concluded the OSA is commonly seen in patients with PTSD. They noted that "patients with PTSD and OSA demonstrated significantly lower adherence to CPAP therapy." There is ample evidence that treating OSA improves PTSD symptoms. In Orr, et. al. (2017) Treatment of OSA with CPAP is Associated with Improvement in PTSD Symptoms Among Veterans; J Clin Sleep Med, 13(1):57-63, the authors describe "a growing body of research has suggested a link between obstructive sleep apnea and PTSD" and "prevalence estimations for OSA in PTSD patients range from 52% to 69%, with some as high as 95%." They note "treatment of OSA with PAP therapy is associated with improvement in PTSD symptoms." They note one factor is that "treatment of OSA with CPAP appears to reduce the frequency of nightmares in PTSD patients." The authors concluded that sleep apnea treatment "should be considered an important component of PTSD treatment for those with concurrent OSA." Psychiatric concerns in general have been noted to be associated with sleep apnea. Rezaeitalab, et. al. (2014) [see The correlation of anxiety and depression with obstructive sleep apnea syndrome, Journal of Research in Medical Sciences, Mar; 19(3): 205–210] studied individuals with obstructive sleep apnea. They found that "53.9% of the individuals had some degree of anxiety, while 46.1% demonstrated depressive symptoms. In terms of OSAS severity, this study showed that OSAS severity was associated with the frequency of anxiety, choking, and sleepiness (P : 0.001). According to polysomnographic results, we found that the majority of patients suffering from anxiety and choking (66.7% and 71.4%, respectively) had severe OSAS." Jehan, et. al. (2017) [see Depression, Obstructive Sleep Apnea and Psychosocial Health, Sleep Med Disord, 1(3): 12] note that "there is a co-linear relationship between" obstructive sleep apnea and depression." Patients with OSA have impaired health and their psychosocial health and daily performance also decrease. They note "because disturbed sleep can cause poor concentration, mood problems, anxiety, and MDD, these factors are also the part of poor daytime performance." Some postulate that weight gain may be a primary cause of sleep apnea, however it is interesting to note that treating sleep apnea with CPAP often actually leads to more weight gain, not less weight gain [see de Milo and Genta (2016), Continuous Positive Airway Pressure and Weight Gain: Do We Know the Mechanisms? American Journal of Respiratory and Critical Care, 194(7): 915]. The research evidence, and the course of the Veteran's disease, support a link between his psychiatric difficulties and sleep apnea.

The Veteran has a diagnosis of obesity. His medical records reflect a BMI in the obese range. A classic but outdated view of OSA is that it is only structural, caused by obstruction of the upper airways and is predominantly found in overweight individuals. The Veteran has a history of concerns related to weight gain. However, it would be an error to suggest that the Veteran's weight gain occurred in a vacuum. Factors associated with his psychiatric disturbance likely significantly contribute to obesity. The scientific literature links psychiatric disturbance to decreased activity and emotional eating which can lead to weight gain. While weight gain potentially contributing to sleep apnea could also likely be due to psychiatric disturbance, it would be an error to rely on opinions that sleep apnea was simply due to being overweight. This is not consistent with the current state of the scientific literature. In fact, neither being overweight nor the presence of structural abnormalities fully explains the presence of sleep apnea in a substantial number of cases. Being overweight is not sufficient to explain the existence of sleep apnea in many individuals. Simply suggesting that OSA was due to being overweight would reflect an overly simplistic and mechanistic view of sleep and obstructive sleep apnea which does not reflect the current state of the science. It would overlook the sleep regulating functions of the brain and the impact of psychiatric disturbance on the sleep regulating functions of the brain, including arousal-based mechanisms associated with sleep apnea. In fact, the scientific literature tells us that "a substantial portion" of patients with obstructive sleep apnea are "not obese" (Gray et. al. 2017). The authors of a 2017 study note that "a substantial proportion of OSA patients are not obese. Non-obese patients with OSA are a challenging group to treat with existing therapies... Our data also indicate that a key nonanatomical contributor to OSA pathogenesis, a low threshold for arousal, is likely to be particularly important in the pathogenesis of OSA in non-obese patients with OSA. A greater propensity for awakening in nonobese patients with OSA may also be a physiological factor contributing, at least in part, to poor CPAP tolerance in these patients. These findings have important implications for the treatment of OSA in nonobese individuals." (Gray, et. al., 2017). In addition, "arousal" plays a significant role in sleep apnea [see Gray, et. al. (2017) Obstructive Sleep Apnea without Obesity Is Common and Difficult to Treat: Evidence for a Distinct Pathophysiological Phenotype; Journal of Clinical Sleep Medicine, 13(1): 81-88]. PTSD is linked to sleep apnea directly, but it is also linked indirectly through weight gain, which is also associated with sleep apnea. PTSD negatively impacts motivation (ex: reducing activity) and can lead to overeating. His PTSD increases the risk for weight gain and obesity, which in turn further increases the risk for obstructive sleep apnea. The Veteran's weight gain occurred in the context of PTSD. Subthreshold and threshold post-traumatic stress disorder (PTSD) are associated with binge eating symptoms in both men and women based on: Braun J, El-Gabalawy R, Sommer JL, Pietrzak RH, Mitchell K, Mota N. Trauma exposure, DSM-5 posttraumatic stress, and binge eating symptoms: results from a nationally representative sample. The Journal of Clinical Psychiatry. 2019;80(6):19m12813. Hoerster, et. al. (2015) noted in "PTSD and depression symptoms are associated with binge eating among US Iraq and Afghanistan veterans" [see Eating Behaviors; Volume 17, April 2015, Pages 115-118] that "PTSD and depression are common conditions among Iraq/Afghanistan Veterans. In the present study, PTSD and depression symptoms were associated with meeting binge eating screening criteria, identifying a possible pathway by which psychiatric conditions lead to disproportionate burden of overweight and obesity in this Veteran cohort." Dorflinger & Masheb (2018), in the research article "PTSD is associated with emotional eating among veterans seeking treatment for overweight/obesity" [see Eating Behaviors, Volume 31, December 2018, Pages 8-11] presented findings that "suggest that emotional eating is common among veterans reporting PTSD symptoms, and that any degree of PTSD symptom severity is associated with more frequent emotional eating." Mental health difficulties can have a significant impact on activity and eating, influencing weight gain. For example, it is notable that major depressive disorder in the DSM-5-TR (pg. 183) lists diagnostic criteria such as "markedly diminished interest or pleasure in all, or almost all, activities most of the day, nearly every day..." and "significant weight loss when not dieting or weight gain (e.g., a change of more than 5% of body weight in a month), or decrease or increase in appetite nearly every day..." and "psychomotor agitation or retardation," and "fatigue or loss of energy nearly every day" and others. PTSD (pg. 302) includes criteria like "markedly diminished interest or participation in significant activities). Overeating and inactivity are symptoms of mental health difficulties which lead to weight gain and obesity. The Veteran's psychiatric difficulties not only directly impacted the Veteran's sleep apnea, but also indirectly by increasing the likelihood of obesity. Mental health difficulties can have a significant impact on activity levels and eating behavior. This can lead to weight gain. For example, it is notable that major depressive disorder in the DSM-5-TR (pg. 183) lists diagnostic criteria such as "markedly diminished interest or pleasure in all, or almost all, activities most of the day, nearly every day..." and "significant weight loss when not dieting or weight gain (e.g., a change of more than 5% of body weight in a month), or decrease or increase in appetite nearly every day..." and "psychomotor agitation or retardation," and "fatigue or loss of energy nearly every day" and others. PTSD (pg. 302) includes criteria like "markedly diminished interest or participation in significant activities). Overeating and inactivity are symptoms of mental health difficulties which lead to weight gain and obesity. The Veteran's psychiatric difficulties not only directly impacted the Veteran's sleep apnea, but also indirectly by increasing the likelihood of obesity. This is still a direct and proximate cause.

The Veteran has service connected alcohol use disorder tied to his PTSD. His treatment records reflect using alcohol in a manner to "self-medicate" his PTSD. The medical literature also demonstrates that alcohol use can make sleep apnea worse. For example, a recent meta-analysis on the topic reviewed 1,266 studies and concluded "alcohol consumption is associated with worsening severity of snoring, altered sleep architecture, AHI, as well as lowest oxygen saturation among patients susceptible to snoring and obstructive sleep apnea" [see Burgos-Sanchez C, Jones NN, Avillion M, Gibson SJ, Patel JA, Neighbors J, Zaghi S, Camacho M. Impact of Alcohol Consumption on Snoring and Sleep Apnea: A Systematic Review and Meta-analysis. Otolaryngol Head Neck Surg. 2020 Dec;163(6):1078-1086]. The American Academy of Sleep Medicine (an organization I am a member of), has practice guidelines related to sleep apnea. The American Academy of Sleep Medicine's practice guidelines related to obstructive sleep apnea include, as a standard of care in the field, that there be "patient education" on the impact of "alcohol avoidance" on sleep apnea. The "avoidance of alcohol" is also included as one of the "behavioral strategies" in managing sleep apnea [for the practice guidelines see Adult Obstructive Sleep Apnea Task Force of the American Academy of Sleep Medicine (2009), Epstein LJ; Kristo D; Strollo PJ; Friedman N; Malhotra A; Patil SP; Ramar K; Rogers R; Schwab RJ; Weaver EM; Weinstein MD. Clinical guideline for the evaluation, management and long-term care of obstructive sleep apnea in adults. J Clin Sleep Med 2009;5(3):263–276]. This reflects a recognition that the alcohol use which is tied to the Veteran's PTSD can substantially aggravate the Veteran's sleep apnea directly (in addition to also leading to a history of excessive caloric intake in the form of alcohol).

The scientific literature supports a direct connection between sleep apnea and arousal associated with psychiatric disturbance, including PTSD. In addition, past VBA decisions have supported this interpretation. The scientific evidence and the Veteran's medical records support a finding that the evidence for sleep apnea being secondary to his PTSD is at least in equipoise. What is established as quite likely is a bidirectional relationship between his psychiatric disturbance and his sleep apnea where each substantially aggravates the other, and that his sleep apnea was initially directly and proximately caused by his psychiatric difficulties. There is research evidence supporting a direct cause for sleep apnea associated with the arousal related to psychiatric disturbance. In this regard, based on the mechanism of hyper-arousal associated with both his psychiatric disturbance and sleep apnea, it is at least as likely as not that his sleep apnea is secondary to his service-connected psychiatric disturbance. Multiple recent VBA decisions have been decided favorably based on this scientific literature, including, but not limited to: Citation Nr: 19133904 (Docket NO. 18-05 0350 5/1/2019; Citation Nr: 19164013 (Docket NO. 15-12 470) 8/19/19; Citation Nr: 19136285 (Docket NO. 18-01 222) 5/10/19; Citation Nr: 20011070 (Docket NO. 19-05 577) 2/10/2020; Citation Nr: 19155477 (Docket NO. 18-28 822) 7/18/19; Citation Nr: 19107744 (Docket NO. 16-51 926) 2/1/19; Citation Nr: 19103608 (Docket NO. 17-05 487) 1/15/19; Citation Nr. 19144930 (Docket NO. 17-49 916) 6/11/19; Citation Nr: 19141163 (DOCKET NO. 18-18 750A) 5/29/19; Citation Nr: 19110858 (Docket NO 16-53 449), 2/12/19). This is not an exhaustive list. This interpretation of the scientific literature should be utilized in favor of the Veteran as it would be arbitrary and capricious for the VA to treat the science differently for one Veteran over another and say the science says one thing for one Veteran but says the opposite for another Veteran.

Conclusions: There is a link between his sleep apnea and his military service. It is at least as likely as not (a 50 percent chance or greater) that the Veteran's sleep apnea is due to the psychiatric difficulties from his military service. His mental health concerns have created hyperarousal and other physiological issues including a risk for weight gain and obesity which in turn directly and proximately cause his sleep apnea while also substantially aggravating and worsening the course and severity of the disease. The Veteran's sleep apnea is at least as likely as not (a 50 percent chance or greater) substantially aggravated by his service-connected PTSD. His PTSD creates chronic sleep impairments which substantially impact the progression and treatment of his sleep apnea. The issue is medically complex, as it requires knowledge of the interaction between multiple systems in the body. I am a psychologist with extensive training related to posttraumatic stress disorder and other psychiatric conditions; I am also trained in Behavioral Sleep Medicine and am a member of the American Academy of Sleep Medicine and the Society of Behavioral Sleep Medicine. The research supports the presence of a significant connection between psychiatric difficulties and sleep apnea, including an arousal-based mechanism initiated by PTSD that promotes the development of sleep apnea in trauma survivors. His PTSD has caused a significant and substantial progression and increased severity of his sleep apnea above and beyond the natural progression of the disease. His sleep apnea is secondary to PTSD; his PTSD significantly contributed to the development of his sleep apnea and has also substantially aggravated his sleep apnea. In turn, his sleep apnea also worsens his psychiatric difficulties to include PTSD. He has chronic sleep impairment impacting his functioning; his mental health concerns and sleep apnea concerns aggravate each other and worsen his functioning. In addition, the scientific literature supports a direct, causal connection between PTSD and sleep apnea. He did not have sleep apnea prior to his PTSD and all impairment associated with it is due to the aggravation from his PTSD. Due to the negative impact on sleep, weight gain and treatment adherence, his sleep apnea and mental health concerns are also likely to delay, impede and/or prevent treatment of each of the conditions, including effective treatment for his mental health concerns. He did not have sleep apnea prior to his mental health concerns. It should be noted that his sleep apnea was directly and proximately caused by his mental health concerns. There is no indication that it existed prior to the onset of his mental health concerns. However, in addition to causing his sleep apnea, his sleep apnea and mental health concerns will now continue to aggravate each other substantially (sleep apnea was not a pre-existing condition to his mental health concerns, his sleep apnea is due to his mental health concerns).

[signature]

Todd Finnerty, Psy.D.
Ohio psychologist #5979
100 E. Campus View Boulevard
Suite #250
Columbus, Ohio 43235

http://www.toddfinnerty.com/CV.docx

Dr. Todd Finnerty is a psychologist in private practice in Columbus, Ohio. He has significant training related to PTSD, including VA-specific training through the contractors VES and QTC. Dr. Finnerty has had the same amount of training or more training than the third-party contractors used by the VA. In the past Dr. Finnerty has performed hundreds of examinations on veterans for VA third-party contractors. Dr. Finnerty also helps make decisions on Social Security disability claims for the state of Ohio and has substantial experience in evaluating impairment. In this role Dr. Finnerty was named the 2012 "Disability Review Physician of the Year" by the National Association of Disability Examiners, Great Lakes Region and the 2010 "Consultant of the Year" by the Ohio Association of Disability Examiners. He has training in behavioral sleep medicine and is a member of the American Academy of Sleep Medicine and the Society of Behavioral Sleep Medicine. Dr. Finnerty is a forensic specialist and adheres to the American Psychological Association's Ethical Principles of Psychologists and Code of Conduct as well as the APA's Specialty Guidelines for Forensic Psychology (https://www.apa.org/practice/guidelines/forensic-psychology). These guidelines include the responsibilities of integrity, impartiality and fairness and note: "When offering expert opinions to be relied upon by a decision maker, providing forensic therapeutic services, or teaching or conducting research, forensic practitioners strive for accuracy, impartiality, fairness, and independence. Forensic practitioners recognize the adversarial nature of the legal system and strive to treat all participants and weigh all data, opinions, and rival hypotheses impartially. When conducting forensic examinations, forensic practitioners strive to be unbiased and impartial, and avoid partisan presentation of unrepresentative, incomplete, or inaccurate evidence that might mislead finders of fact. This guideline does not preclude forceful presentation of the data and reasoning upon which a conclusion or professional product is based." While it would be convenient if Veterans in need of first or second opinions on mental health related claims could seek them from treatment providers at the VA, VA policy outlined in VHA Directive 1134(2) Provision of Medical Statements and Completion of Forms by VA Health Care Providers recommends that VA mental health treatment providers not complete forms such as "mental health DBQ's" in order to "maintain the integrity of the patient-provider relationship." Therefore, both the VA and Veterans often must seek forensic specialists outside of a treatment relationship to provide opinions related to their case.

OTHER INTERESTING RESEARCH ARTICLE LINKS FOR A DEEPER DIVE:

- Sforza E, Addati G, Cirignotta F, Lugaresi E. Natural evolution of sleep apnoea syndrome: a five year longitudinal study. *Eur Respir J.* 1994;7:1765–1770.
- Berry & Gleason (1997) Respiratory arousal from sleep: mechanisms and significance; Sleep 20(8):654-75.
- Edwards, et. al. (2014) Clinical predictors of the respiratory arousal threshold in patients with obstructive sleep apnea; Am J Respir Crit Care Med 2014 Dec 1;190(11):1293-300
- Malhotra, et. al. (2020) Endotypes and phenotypes in obstructive sleep apnea; Curr Opin Pulm Med 2020 Nov;26(6):609-614
- Liempt, et. al. (2013) Sympathetic activity and hypothalamo-pituitary-adrenal axis activity during sleep in post-traumatic stress disorder: a study assessing polysomnography with simultaneous blood sampling; Psychoneuroendocrinology Jan;38(1):155-65

- Koob (1999) Corticotropin-releasing factor, norepinephrine, and stress; Biol Psychiatry Nov 1;46(9):1167-80
- Block, et. al. (2009) Psychosocial stress and change in weight among US adults; Jul 15;170(2):181-92
- Lettieri, et. al. (2016) OSA Syndrome and Posttraumatic Stress Disorder: Clinical Outcomes and Impact of Positive Airway Pressure Therapy; Chest 149(2):483-490
- El-Solh, et al. (2017) The effect of continuous positive airway pressure on post-traumatic stress disorder symptoms in veterans with post-traumatic stress disorder and obstructive sleep apnea: a prospective study. Sleep Med ;33: 145-150
- Lechat et. al. (2021) Co-morbid insomnia and obstructive sleep apnoea is associated with all-cause mortality; European Respiratory Journal, DOI: 10.1183/13993003.01958-2021
- Chang WH, Wu HC, Lan CC, Wu YK, Yang MC (2021) The Worsening of Positional Mild Obstructive Sleep Apnea over Time Is Associated with an Increase in Body Weight: Impact on Blood Pressure and Autonomic Nervous System. Respiration. 2021;100(11):1060-1069.
- Pevernagie DA, Gnidovec-Strazisar B, Grote L, Heinzer R, McNicholas WT, Penzel T, Randerath W, Schiza S, Verbraecken J, Arnardottir ES. On the rise and fall of the apnea-hypopnea index: A historical review and critical appraisal. J Sleep Res. 2020 Aug;29(4):e13066. doi: 10.1111/

jsr.13066. Epub 2020 May 14. PMID: 32406974.

THE SLEEP APNEA DBQ AND FUNCTIONAL IMPAIRMENT

In the context of a VA disability claim, DBQ stands for disability benefits questionnaire. A DBQ is a standard form the VA uses which is completed by C&P examiners to report information the VA uses to rate the level of impairment of disorders. Nexus opinions are commonly offered as a separate independent medical opinion from the DBQ; a nexus opinion isn't usually the central aim of a DBQ. Most DBQ's typically aren't focused on providing the medical opinion or information for establishing a nexus to service itself- that typically occurs separately as an independent medical opinion. You can pay for a private DBQ, and some Veterans think this might help them get a faster decision, but it is important to be aware that this is the same information that a C&P examiner would collect and report during an exam. If the VA sends you to a C&P exam a DBQ would be completed by the C&P examiner at no cost to you. As always there are no guarantees; the VA may still send you to a C&P examination even if you pay for a private DBQ.

There is a publicly available version of many DBQ's on the

VA's website. These DBQ forms are similar to the DBQ's completed by C&P examiners (though not all of the DBQ's are listed on the VA's website; for example, at the time of this writing there is no Initial PTSD DBQ listed publicly on the website, only a review PTSD DBQ- the Initial PTSD DBQ is a more detailed DBQ that is completed the first time a Veteran is examined for PTSD by a C&P examiner). The publicly available DBQ's are listed here: **https:// www.benefits.va.gov/compensation/ dbq_publicdbqs.asp**

The VA's website for the publicly available DBQ's notes *"it is intended that the DBQs will be completed by the Veteran's health care provider."* As of this writing the publicly available DBQ's also ask questions like:

- Are you a VA Healthcare provider?
- Is the Veteran regularly seen as a patient in your clinic?
- Was the Veteran examined in person?

The questions about whether the DBQ was completed by a VA healthcare provider and if they are regularly seen as a patient in your clinic are relevant but could be unfairly misused by a VA decisionmaker and are somewhat disingenuous given other VA policies. While it would be convenient if Veterans in need of first or second opinions on mental health related claims could seek them from treatment providers at the VA, VA policy outlined in *VHA Directive 1134(2) Provision of Medical Statements and Completion of Forms by VA Health Care Providers* recommends that VA mental health treatment providers not complete forms such as "mental health DBQ's" in order to "maintain the integrity of the patient-provider relationship," for example. As noted in the section about ethics and forensic professionals, treatment providers may be inclined to defer to forensic examiners as they may lack or expertise or the desire to have the disability claim impact the "patient-provider relationship." Therefore, both the VA and Veterans often must seek forensic specialists outside of a treatment relationship to provide opinions related to their case.

Sleep apnea leads to functional impairment and CPAP can help with this functional impairment, however, it is a misconception that CPAP/ PAP therapy is expected to resolve all impairments for an individual with sleep apnea; this is not consistent with the scientific evidence. In addition, the AHI is not a reliable measure for all of the functional impairment associated with sleep apnea. Some relevant information from the scientific literature includes (but is not limited to):

OSA "impairs quality of life for numerous patients and leads to various OSA complications." The authors noted that "the role of serotonin (5-HT) in many physiological processes, studies on its connection with the circadian system, and relationship to changes in sleep architecture are insufficient to assess the interaction of this neurotransmitter with nocturnal hypoxia," but they did find that treatment with PAP therapy did lead to an increase in serotonin levels in individuals with sleep apnea [Madaeva IM, Berdina ON, Kurashova NA, Semenova NV, Ukhinov EB, Belskikh AV, Kolesnikova LI. Sleep Apnea and Serum Serotonin Level Pre- and Post-PAP Therapy: A Preliminary Study. Neurol Ther. 2021 Dec;10(2):1095-1102. doi: 10.1007/s40120-021-00290-z. Epub 2021 Oct 20].

We know that sleep apnea leads to "an increase in occupational accidents due to reduced vigilance and attention" in individuals with sleep apnea. "Such involvements were related to excessive daytime sleepiness and neurocognitive function impairments" [see Rabelo Guimarães Mde L, Hermont AP. Sleep apnea and occupational accidents: Are oral appliances the solution? Indian J Occup Environ Med. 2014 May;18(2):39-47]. We know that "cognitive impairments are commonly seen in patients with an OSA diagnosis" [see Wang G, Goebel JR, Li C, Hallman HG, Gilford TM, Li W. Therapeutic effects of CPAP on cognitive impairments associated with OSA. J Neurol. 2020 Oct;267(10):2823-2828. doi: 10.1007/s00415-019-09381-2. Epub 2019 May 20. PMID: 31111204]. "One of the major consequences of OSAS is an impact on neurocognitive functioning. Several studies have shown that OSAS has an adverse effect on inductive and deductive reasoning, attention, vigilance, learning, and memory" [see Lal C, Strange C, Bachman D. Neurocognitive impairment in obstructive sleep apnea. Chest. 2012 Jun;141(6):1601-1610].

Jackson, et. al. (2018) treated 110 patients with OSA with CPAP for three months and compared them to individuals in the community without OSA. "Compared to the community sample, participants with OSA were significantly sleepier, had impaired mood and quality of life, and showed decrements in neuropsychological function, specifically psychomotor function, working memory and vigilance. Some neuropsychological and mood outcomes were normalized with CPAP, but significant decrements persisted in most outcomes even in those participants with adequate device usage." The authors found that "Patients with mild to moderate OSA have significant neurobehavioral morbidity. During "gold standard" treatment, normal function was not achieved, even with adequate device usage. CPAP efficacy for improving sleepiness and neuropsychological function in this milder end of the OSA spectrum may be poor, which may affect CPAP adherence. These findings suggest that there may be neurological changes related to OSA that do not respond to CPAP treatment. [see Jackson ML, McEvoy RD, Banks S, Barnes M. Neurobehavioral Impairment and CPAP Treatment Response in Mild-Moderate Obstructive Sleep Apneas. J Clin Sleep Med. 2018 Jan 15;14(1):47-56].

Jiang, et, al. (2021) completed a metanalysis of multiple studies and found that sleep apnea is associated with "high risks of cognitive impairment, including Alzheimer's disease" and that CPAP only offers "partial" improvement in the cognitive problems caused by sleep apnea [see Jiang X, Wang Z, Hu N, Yang Y, Xiong R, Fu Z. Cognition effectiveness of continuous positive airway pressure treatment in obstructive sleep apnea syndrome patients with cognitive impairment: a meta-analysis. Exp Brain Res. 2021 Dec;239(12):3537-3552].

Kielb, et. al. (2012) also note that OSA is "associated with a number of adverse health consequences, and a growing literature focuses on its cognitive correlates." They note that "multiple studies indicate" that individuals with OSA "show impairment in attention, memory, and executive function." While CPAP was the "most effective and widely used treatment" for sleep apnea, the studies of CPAP use showed that "in general, no consistent effect of CPAP use on cognitive performance was evident." The authors noted also that "several prior reviews of the literature suggested that OSAS patients exhibit significant impairment on neuropsychological tests." They reviewed evidence that OSA patients are "are at increased risk for motor vehicle accidents." The reviewed multiple studies with mixed results and design. While some research shows some potential cognitive improvement with CPAP use, they noted that "in fact, several studies have reported that CPAP treatment has no effect on cognitive performance." The authors concluded that "cognitive deficits have long been observed in OSAS patients, and although findings in this domain remain inconsistent, evidence exists for deficits in intellectual function, memory, attention, and executive function in OSAS." Due to the mixed results of treatment studies, which may be due to variability in inclusion and exclusion criteria, study design, and duration of treatment, it is not possible to make definitive conclusions regarding the impact of CPAP treatment on cognition in OSAS. Although CPAP is a well-established, effective treatment for OSAS, it does not definitively reduce the host of cognitive deficits observed among OSAS patients. Daytime somnolence can particularly impact attention and executive functioning, including slower reaction time. Intermittent hypoxemia also can impact the performance on cognitive tests and is associated with declines in motor and processing speed, spatial abilities, mental flexibility and attention. "Some researchers argue that intermittent hypoxemia, together with sleep fragmentation, leads to prefrontal cortical degeneration, which could explain the impairment in executive function observed in patients" with OSA. Sleep fragmentation itself may be "an important mechanistic factor in the development of cognitive impairment" in sleep apnea. "For example, the number of arousals from sleep is a strong predictor of memory impairment in OSAS." Sleep fragmentation has been associated with poorer cognitive performance and reduction in neurogenesis. "Another potential mechanism that may contribute to cognitive impairment in OSAS is disruption in circadian rhythms. Researchers have reported an association between disturbed circadian rhythms (as measured by actigraphy) and severity of cognitive impairment" [see Kielb SA, Ancoli-Israel S, Rebok GW, Spira AP. Cognition in obstructive sleep apnea-hypopnea syndrome (OSAS): current clinical knowledge and the impact of treatment. Neuromolecular Med. 2012 Sep;14(3):180-93. doi: 10.1007/s12017-012-8182-1. Epub 2012 May 9].

COMMENTS ON THE 2022 PROPOSED CHANGES TO THE VA SLEEP APNEA RATING

In 2022 the VA proposed dramatic changes for how impairment from sleep apnea is rated (which sadly may have the unintended consequence of incentivizing noncompliance with a treatment that can be hard to adjust to and comply with, i.e. PAP therapy such as a CPAP). You can view that here: *Federal Register :: Schedule for Rating Disabilities-Ear, Nose, Throat, and Audiology Disabilities; Special Provisions Regarding Evaluation of Respiratory Conditions; Schedule for Rating Disabilities-Respiratory System* [see https://www.federalregister.gov/documents/2022/02/15/2022-02049/schedule-for-rating-disabilities-ear-nose-throat-and-audiology-disabilities-special-provisions].

Here is an excerpt related to sleep apnea:

VA also proposes to modernize the rating criteria for DC 6847, "Sleep Apnea Syndromes (Obstructive, Central, Mixed)" and retitle that DC as "Sleep Apnea Syndromes (Obstructive, Central, or Mixed)". The discipline of sleep medicine has greatly evolved since VA published the existing criteria. The American Academy of Sleep Medicine (AASM), founded since then, conducted in-depth, peer-reviewed research in conjunction with its partners to develop scientifically-refined criteria regarding the definition, measurement, and treatment of sleep apnea. Sleep apnea may be defined as complaints of unintentional sleep episodes and/or awakenings and/or snoring associated with an apnea-hypopnea index (AHI) equal to or greater than 5 per hour or, alternatively, an asymptomatic patient with an AHI greater than 15 per hour. See Richard B. Berry, Fundamentals of Sleep Medicine 238 (2012). Additional findings supporting a diagnosis of sleep apnea include oxygen desaturation greater than 4 percent and/or a reduction in airflow below 70 percent. Such measurements can evaluate the effectiveness of treatment intervention or lifestyle modifications such as weight loss.

VA proposes to extensively revise the rating criteria for sleep apnea to primarily provide compensation that is more compatible with earning impairment than the current criteria. The current criteria evaluate based upon treatment rather than actual impairment. VA currently assigns higher ratings to individuals when their physicians prescribe more intensive therapies, such as continuous airway pressure (CPAP) machines, without regard to whether individuals first tried more conservative therapies, such as weight loss or oral appliances, or what actual impairment continues following use of CPAP machines. As discussed below, VA's proposed criteria will focus on the result rather than the type of treatment. Hence, individuals whose treatments are equally effective will receive equal disability ratings, regardless of the treatments. Individuals for whom treatment similarly fails (or is only partially effective) will also receive similar ratings. These proposed changes for sleep apnea comply with 38 U.S.C.

1155 that the VASRD ratings reflect average losses in earning capacity.

Specifically, VA proposes to assign a 0 percent evaluation when sleep apnea syndrome is asymptomatic, with or without treatment. VA would assign a 10 percent evaluation when treatment yields "incomplete relief." VA would assign ratings above 10 percent (e.g., 50 and 100 percent) only when treatment is either ineffective or the veteran is unable to use the prescribed treatment due to comorbid conditions. VA would assign a 100 percent evaluation only if there is also end-organ damage. VA proposes to include an informational note that defines and gives examples of qualifying comorbid conditions, i.e., conditions that, in the opinion of a qualified medical provider, directly impede or prevent the use of, or implementation of, a recognized form of treatment intervention normally shown to be effective.

6847 Sleep apnea syndromes (obstructive, central, or mixed):

Treatment ineffective (as determined by sleep study) or unable to use treatment due to comorbid conditions; and with end-organ damage
..
..
.... 100
Treatment ineffective (as determined by sleep study) or unable to use treatment due to comorbid conditions; and without end-organ damage
..
..
.... 50
Incomplete relief (as determined by sleep study) with treatment

....

.... *10*

Asymptomatic   with   or   without   treatment

....

.... *0*

Note: Qualifying comorbidities are conditions that, in the opinion of a qualified medical provider, directly impede or prevent the habitual use of a recognized form of treatment shown by sleep study to be effective in the affected veteran's case (e.g., contact dermatitis where the mask or interface touches the face or nares, Parkinson's disease, missing limbs, facial dis-figurement, or skull fracture).

Personally, I'm not a fan of the VA's proposed changes to how sleep apnea is rated. For one, the notation "as determined by sleep study" isn't realistic given that it isn't routine practice for Veterans to keep getting sleep studies over and over again to see how their CPAP is working, and the data from their CPAP itself rarely if ever actually makes it into a medical record (and wouldn't reasonably be considered a sleep study anyway). The data the VA would want wouldn't be available to the Veteran and therefore there'd be an undue burden on them. Regardless, sleep studies in this context would often not yield the data that is most relevant to the continued impairment seen despite CPAP use. For example, the AHI which is a measure obtained in a sleep study and is often used as a shorthand for severity of sleep apnea, is not an ideal predictor of actual functional impairment. Sleep studies also have no measures of the many actual lingering functional impairments tied to sleep apnea such as cognitive impairment (but I don't see where the VA is indicating that they are willing to pay for a neuropsychological evaluation for every single Veteran having continued lingering symptoms despite their CPAP use). There is already a wait for sleep studies so unnecessarily increasing the demand for sleep studies, when those sleep studies don't actually measure the important lingering impairment, will do more harm than good.

Ironically, while the VA is concerned about saving the pennies they are spending on VA disability claims related to sleep apnea, the proposal is pound-foolish. While CPAP use/ breathing assistance device use is not a fool-proof proxy for impairment and loss of earnings potential, there are few other evidence-based contenders to replace it. More importantly, the unique position of CPAP use in the disability rating has created a positive public health phenomenon where Veterans are now educating each other about sleep apnea and supporting each other's pursuit of the gold standard treatment of PAP therapy. This has an incredibly powerful and positive public health impact and preventing all the negative consequences of untreated sleep apnea in Veterans will save the VA money in the long-term despite the money spent on sleep apnea disability claims. CPAP use has been proven to be cost-effective for healthcare systems. However, CPAP is also notoriously hard to adjust to and a huge percentage of individuals prescribed a CPAP do not continue with CPAP use because of that. We also know that individuals with PTSD in particular have difficulties adjusting to the CPAP due to their symptoms. The VA's new proposal would have a profoundly negative impact on Veterans and reverse the course of progress that has been made in identifying Veterans with untreated sleep apnea and increasing their adherence to PAP therapy. The VA's proposal would actually incentivize Veterans to give up on an important treatment that is very difficult to adjust to, leading them to have an increased likelihood of countless other difficulties due to that untreated sleep apnea. This proposal would have a very negative impact on the overall health of Veterans and quite literally kill them more quickly by contributing to their early deaths from the consequences of untreated sleep apnea. The public health benefit of using CPAP/breathing assistance device use as a proxy for impairment and potential income loss (including preventing the early deaths of our Veterans) far outweigh any concerns related to the cost of paying those sleep apnea claims.

This appears supported by recent evidence from another disorder, diabetes. "As policy makers consider potential changes to veteran disability compensation programs, we offer evidence that compensation payments substantially lower hospitalizations to veterans, particularly those financed by Medicare," Trivedi said in a VA news release. "This means that disability compensation may generate important reductions in public spending for hospital care." [See *Amal N. Trivedi et al, Association of Disability Compensation With Mortality and Hospitalizations Among Vietnam-Era Veterans With Diabetes, JAMA Internal Medicine (2022). DOI: 10.1001/ jamainternmed.2022.2159*].

Dr. Finnerty's public comments on the 2022 proposed changes to the VA sleep apnea rating

March 4, 2022

The VA's proposed changes would incentivize failure and drive-up associated healthcare costs and disease burden.

Our Veterans deserve better.

A Penny-wise but Pound-foolish Proposal

I disagree with the VA's proposed changes to how sleep apnea is rated for disability claims. Ironically, while the VA is concerned about saving the pennies they are spending on VA disability claims related to sleep apnea, the proposal is pound-foolish. While CPAP use/ breathing assistance device use is not a fool-proof proxy for impairment and loss of earnings potential, there are few other evidence-based contenders to replace it. More importantly, the unique position of CPAP use in the disability rating has created a positive public health phenomenon where Veterans are now educating each other about sleep apnea and supporting each other's pursuit of the gold standard treatment of PAP therapy. This has an incredibly powerful and positive public health impact; preventing all the negative consequences of untreated sleep apnea in Veterans will save the VA money in the long-term despite the money spent on sleep apnea disability claims. CPAP use has been proven to be cost-effective for healthcare systems. However, CPAP is also notoriously hard to adjust to and a huge percentage of individuals prescribed a CPAP do not continue with CPAP use because of that. We also know that individuals with PTSD and other mental health conditions in particular have difficulties adjusting to PAP therapy due to their symptoms. The VA's new proposal would have a profoundly negative impact on Veterans and reverse the course of progress that has been made in identifying Veterans with untreated sleep apnea and increasing their adherence to PAP therapy. The VA's ill-considered proposal would actually incentivize Veterans to give up on an important treatment that is very difficult to adjust to, leading them to have an increased likelihood of countless other difficulties due to that untreated sleep apnea. This proposal would have a very negative impact on the overall health of Veterans and quite literally kill them more quickly by contributing to their early deaths from the consequences of untreated sleep apnea. The public health benefit of using CPAP/breathing assistance device use as a proxy for impairment and potential income loss (including preventing the early deaths of our Veterans) far outweigh any concerns related to the cost of paying those sleep apnea claims. "As Determined by a Sleep Study" fails to capture actual functional impairment I disagree with the use of "as determined by a sleep study" in the rating criteria. The notation "as determined by sleep study" to decide whether treatment is effective isn't realistic given that it isn't routine practice for Veterans to keep getting sleep studies over and over again to see how their CPAP or other treatment is working, and the data from their CPAP rarely ever actually makes it into a medical record (and can't reasonably be considered a sleep study anyway). The data the VA would want wouldn't be available to the Veteran or the C&P examiner and therefore there'd be an undue burden on Todd Finnerty, Psy.D. Ohio Psychologist #5979 NPI: 1427266741 www.toddfinnerty.com www.NexusLetters.com 2 the Veteran making it nearly impossible for them to prove their claim in most instances. In addition, it would create a push to keep providing sleep studies over and over again which were not medically necessary, simply to help provide Veterans with evidence for their disability claims. It would divert precious sleep study utilization to Veterans seeking more data for their disability claims and worsen the backlog for Veterans who need to be evaluated for sleep apnea for the first time. Regardless, sleep studies often do not yield the data that is most relevant to the continued impairment seen despite CPAP use. For example, the AHI which is a measure obtained in a sleep study and is often used as a shorthand for severity of sleep apnea, is not an ideal predictor of actual functional impairment and has been much criticized in the medical literature. Pevernagie, et. al. (2020) offer a review on the data related to the AHI, the metric most-likely to be looked at by inexperienced C&P examiners when addressing whether treatment was effective "as determined by a sleep study." The AHI "has been criticized for not capturing relevant clinical features of obstructive sleep apnea." The authors note "the lack of evidence has become sufficiently robust to accept that clinically relevant OSA cannot be ruled in or out based on the sole use of the AHI. In fact, the AHI fails to indicate a disease state or its severity in the individual OSA patient. This conclusion is supported not only by the various trials showing a flimsy correlation of the AHI with symptom scores and associated co-morbid conditions, but also because the AHI has been found to explain no more than 25% of the variance in relevant outcomes such as driving performance and sleepiness..." The authors note "the widely accepted severity cut-offs 5, 15 and 30 per [hour], introduced in the Chicago criteria, are invalid. It has been emphasized over and over again that these severity categories are arbitrary and misleading for clinical decision-making... Ergo, AHI should be abandoned as a "stand alone" exposure variable of clinically relevant SDB in the individual OSA patient." The authors note that "this is actually bad news for all the organizations that rely on AHI cut-offs for decision-making" [see Pevernagie DA, Gnidovec-Strazisar B, Grote L, Heinzer R, McNicholas WT,

Penzel T, Randerath W, Schiza S, Verbraecken J, Arnardottir ES. On the rise and fall of the apnea-hypopnea index: A historical review and critical appraisal. J Sleep Res. 2020 Aug;29(4):e13066. doi: 10.1111/jsr.13066. Epub 2020 May 14. PMID: 32406974]. Given that the field is moving away from using sleep study measures like the AHI as a proxy for impairment, the VA should not burden Veterans with this non-evidence based proposed impairment rating system. Even if a follow up sleep study was done related to the impact of treatment on the AHI (despite a lack of sufficient ties to actual functional impairment from this measure), this is just a limited snapshot in time. The measure can vary significantly based on a variety of factors. It also does not consider the fact that sometimes individuals undergoing a sleep study have difficulty sleeping; this difficulty sleeping means an increased possibility that their events won't be sufficiently captured in the study, or the metrics obtained were not reflective of a typical night. Therefore, issues like insomnia and PTSD leading to them failing to sleep sufficiently during the study could potentially lead to metrics on the study which would imply that their treatment for sleep apnea was actually working well when it wasn't. Metrics like the AHI could therefore be deceptive in settings where an individual with PTSD or insomnia was not able to sleep (because the Veteran had not entered the sleep state long enough to have sufficient apnea and/or hypopnea events recorded). Sleep studies also have no measures of the many actual lingering functional impairments tied to sleep apnea such as cognitive impairment. The VA suggested treatment being ineffective "as determined by a sleep study," but I don't see where the VA is indicating that they are willing to consider the results of neuropsychological examinations or pay for a neuropsychological evaluation for every single Veteran having continued lingering cognitive symptoms despite their CPAP use (and presumably the VA wouldn't want to keep sending them to sleep studies for disability purposes either). Given the increasing use of auto-CPAP it is becoming less and less common for individuals to even have an attended CPAP titration 3 study let alone additional full sleep studies to evaluate their treatment effectiveness, so the data related to ongoing impairment is not likely to be available in Veterans' medical records. Sleep apnea leads to functional impairment and CPAP can help with this functional impairment; however, it is a misconception that CPAP/ PAP therapy is expected to resolve all impairments for an individual with sleep apnea; this is not consistent with the scientific evidence. In addition, the AHI is not a reliable measure for all of the functional impairment associated with sleep apnea. Some relevant information from the scientific literature related to other factors not seen on a sleep study includes (but is not limited to): We know that sleep apnea leads to "an increase in occupational accidents due to reduced vigilance and attention" in individuals with sleep apnea. "Such involvements were related to excessive daytime sleepiness and neurocognitive function impairments" [see Rabelo Guimarães Mde L, Hermont AP. Sleep apnea and occupational accidents: Are oral appliances the solution? Indian J Occup Environ Med. 2014 May;18(2):39-47]. We know that "cognitive impairments are commonly seen in patients with an OSA diagnosis" [see Wang G, Goebel JR, Li C, Hallman HG, Gilford TM, Li W. Therapeutic effects of CPAP on cognitive impairments associated with OSA. J Neurol. 2020 Oct;267(10):2823-2828. doi: 10.1007/

s00415-019-09381-2. Epub 2019 May 20. PMID: 31111204]. "One of the major consequences of OSAS is an impact on neurocognitive functioning. Several studies have shown that OSAS has an adverse effect on inductive and deductive reasoning, attention, vigilance, learning, and memory" [see Lal C, Strange C, Bachman D. Neurocognitive impairment in obstructive sleep apnea. Chest. 2012 Jun;141(6):1601-1610]. Jackson, et. al. (2018) treated 110 patients with OSA with CPAP for three months and compared them to individuals in the community without OSA. "Compared to the community sample, participants with OSA were significantly sleepier, had impaired mood and quality of life, and showed decrements in neuropsychological function, specifically psychomotor function, working memory and vigilance. Some neuropsychological and mood outcomes were normalized with CPAP, but significant decrements persisted in most outcomes even in those participants with adequate device usage." The authors found that "Patients with mild to moderate OSA have significant neurobehavioral morbidity. During "gold standard" treatment, normal function was not achieved, even with adequate device usage. CPAP efficacy for improving sleepiness and neuropsychological function in this milder end of the OSA spectrum may be poor, which may affect CPAP adherence. These findings suggest that there may be neurological changes related to OSA that do not respond to CPAP treatment. [see Jackson ML, McEvoy RD, Banks S, Barnes M. Neurobehavioral Impairment and CPAP Treatment Response in Mild-Moderate Obstructive Sleep Apneas. J Clin Sleep Med. 2018 Jan 15;14(1):47-56]. Jiang, et, al. (2021) completed a metanalysis of multiple studies and found that sleep apnea is associated with "high risks of cognitive impairment, including Alzheimer's disease" and that CPAP only offers "partial" improvement in the cognitive problems caused by sleep apnea [see Jiang X, Wang Z, Hu N, Yang Y, Xiong R, Fu Z. Cognition effectiveness of continuous positive airway pressure treatment in obstructive sleep apnea syndrome patients with cognitive impairment: a meta-analysis. Exp Brain Res. 2021 Dec;239(12):3537-3552]. Kielb, et. al. (2012) also note that OSA is "associated with a number of adverse health consequences, and a growing literature focuses on its cognitive correlates." They note that "multiple studies indicate" that individuals with OSA "show impairment in attention, memory, 4 and executive function." While CPAP was the "most effective and widely used treatment" for sleep apnea, the studies of CPAP use showed that "in general, no consistent effect of CPAP use on cognitive performance was evident." The authors noted also that "several prior reviews of the literature suggested that OSAS patients exhibit significant impairment on neuropsychological tests." They reviewed evidence that OSA patients are "are at increased risk for motor vehicle accidents." The reviewed multiple studies with mixed results and design. While some research shows some potential cognitive improvement with CPAP use, they noted that "in fact, several studies have reported that CPAP treatment has no effect on cognitive performance." The authors concluded that "cognitive deficits have long been observed in OSAS patients, and although findings in this domain remain inconsistent, evidence exists for deficits in intellectual function, memory, attention, and executive function in OSAS." Due to the mixed results of treatment studies, which may be due to variability in inclusion and exclusion criteria, study design, and duration of treatment, it is not possible to make definitive conclusions regarding the impact of CPAP treatment on cognition in OSAS. Although CPAP is a wellestablished, effective treatment for OSAS, it does not definitively reduce the host of cognitive deficits observed among OSAS patients. Daytime somnolence can particularly impact attention and executive functioning, including slower reaction time. Intermittent hypoxemia also can impact the performance on cognitive tests and is associated with declines in motor and processing speed, spatial abilities, mental flexibility and attention. "Some researchers argue that intermitted hypoxemia, together with sleep fragmentation, leads to prefrontal cortical degeneration, which could explain the impairment in executive function observed in patients" with OSA. Sleep fragmentation itself may be "an important mechanistic factor in the development of cognitive impairment" in sleep apnea. "For example, the number of arousals from sleep is a strong predictor of memory impairment in OSAS." Sleep fragmentation has been associated with poorer cognitive performance and reduction in neurogenesis. "Another potential mechanism that may contribute to cognitive impairment in OSAS is disruption in circadian rhythms. Researchers have reported an association between disturbed circadian rhythms (as measured by actigraphy) and severity of cognitive impairment" [see Kielb SA, AncoliIsrael S, Rebok GW, Spira AP. Cognition in obstructive sleep apnea-hypopnea syndrome (OSAS): current clinical knowledge and the impact of treatment. Neuromolecular Med. 2012 Sep;14(3):180-93. doi: 10.1007/s12017-012-8182-1. Epub 2012 May 9]. The evidence reflects significant functional deficits may persist despite CPAP treatment. The evidence also reflects that a sleep study, including the AHI result, does not reliably measure these deficits. A sleep study will not reliably predict the impact on a Veteran's earnings power or the extent to which CPAP has made them whole in relation to the impact on their relationships, community functioning and increased likelihood of "serious complications such as heart attack, glaucoma, diabetes, cancer, and cognitive and behavioral disorders" per the NIH [see https://www.nhlbi.nih.gov/health-topics/sleep-apnea]. Stay the course on identifying and treating sleep apnea in the Veteran population The VA should do nothing and make no changes to the current disability rating structure for disability related to sleep apnea. There are no evidence-based alternatives, and the current proposal will actually harm the overall health of the Veteran population. By making no changes on this proposal the VA will save the time, confusion, and money they would have spent proliferating new DBQ's, training raters and C&P examiners and confronting the chaos caused by having two different rating approaches to deal with on sleep apnea (as Veterans who had a C&P based on the old DBQ could not possibly be rated fairly under the new system). The VA will also reap the benefits of the extensive cost savings on the healthcare side as treating sleep apnea appropriately prevents much costlier healthcare difficulties 5 down the road. We'll reap the cost-effective, significant public health benefits of having an informed population of Veterans who are motivated to educate each other about sleep apnea and motivated to encourage each other to stick with their PAP therapy. The VA's current disability rating structure for sleep apnea should continue as there is nothing evidence based to replace it with, and it also serves as a cost-effective public health campaign promoting the identification of sleep apnea and adherence to gold standard treatment with PAP therapy. The VA's proposed changes would incentivize failure and drive-up associated healthcare costs and disease burden. Our Veterans deserve better.

WHAT ARE YOUR CHANCES OF HAVING A CLAIM APPROVED FOR SLEEP APNEA SECONDARY TO PTSD?

Truthfully, I don't have good statistics related to the percentage of claims for sleep apnea secondary to PTSD that get approved on the first attempt. However, if your VA disability claim for sleep apnea secondary to PTSD is denied but then goes to BVA, and BVA makes an allowance or denial decision (rather than a remand), it is at least as likely as not that your denial will be overturned and your case will be approved (based on a 102 case analysis from early 2022 conducted by Dr. Finnerty). Even though claims may have been denied more than once in the past, when the claim gets to BVA it can be a coin flip in relation to whether a decision is an approval. Given that they were denied in the past, this is actually good odds. The fact that there is such a large percentage of these denials getting overturned at BVA should be considered a significant issue for the

VA given that we'd like to see correct approval decisions for Veterans earlier in the application process. Also note that this includes the decisions for Veterans who never obtained a nexus letter (presumably these cases may be more likely to be denied again if the only opinion is a negative one from a C&P examiner). The quality of the available evidence differs from case to case.

The "at least as likely as not" statement above should be taken with a grain of salt. It is based on a limited run of data from early 2022. Dr. Finnerty took the first 102 relevant cases that came up on a search he conducted on BVA's website; the cases were from the early months of 2022. Dr. Finnerty entered the terms sleep apnea and PTSD using the "search decisions" button on VBA's website (https://www.bva.va.gov/) and then looked for cases where there was an allowance or denial (not a remand) related to sleep apnea being secondary to PTSD. Remands were not included. Denials where the Veteran was clearly not applying secondary to PTSD or another psych condition were not included, nor were approvals where PTSD or other psychological conditions were clearly not in the rationale. Also, in terms of denials, it is notable that there are a not-insignificant number of times when Veterans are being denied for service connection for sleep apnea at the BVA level where they have literally never had a sleep study or sleep apnea diagnosis (it is not clear if they were hoping to have the VA send them to a sleep study in order to see if they had sleep apnea, but it is likely that they were hoping the VA would send them to a first-time sleep study to see if they had sleep apnea and they never received that sleep study- just denial decisions and a long wait). There are also times when Veterans apply secondary to psychological conditions which have not yet been service connected which negatively impacts the fate of the sleep apnea claim if they do not get service connected. If their PTSD does not become service connected then there is no hope for sleep apnea secondary to a not service connected PTSD. There were also a number of claims where Veterans were given direct service connections despite no evidence from service, and where PTSD was clearly considered in the decision yet conclusions were made such as "since the Board is granting this claim on the premise of direct incurrence of this condition during the Veteran's service, favorable resolution of this claim ultimately does not turn on whether the sleep apnea instead is secondary to his already determined to be service-connected PTSD meaning caused or aggravated by it. He only needs to establish his entitlement on one basis to prevail, which he has" (ex: see Citation Nr: 22025433). These were not included. While these types of approvals shouldn't be expected, they emphasize that lay statements of people who observed your sleep apnea symptoms during military service may not be medical evidence, but they can be compelling evidence when combined with post-military supporting medical evidence and research citations. If you have people who witnessed sleep apnea symptoms from you while in the military, it makes sense to get buddy letters from them. While typically this wouldn't be sufficient, it can help.

In the interest of open science and transparency, here are the decisions used for this particular analysis. Out of 102 BVA cases from early 2022 related to sleep apnea secondary to PTSD there were 51 approvals (y) and 51 denials (n):

Citation number	granted y/n
Citation Nr: A22007315	y
Citation Nr: A22006831	n
Citation Nr: 22020381	n
Citation Nr: 22014071	y
Citation Nr: 22022148	n
Citation Nr: 22004919	n
Citation Nr: 22002762	n
Citation Nr: A22007648	n
Citation Nr: A22001989	y
Citation Nr: 22009389	n
Citation Nr: 22015892	y
Citation Nr: A22002833	y
Citation Nr: 22022539	n
Citation Nr: 22005398	n
Citation Nr: 22011689	n
Citation Nr: A22006090	n
Citation Nr: 22009908	y
Citation Nr: 22017291	n
Citation Nr: 22004808	n
Citation Nr: 22015892	y
Citation Nr: 22002762	n
Citation Nr: A22001093	n
Citation Nr: A22006012	n
Citation Nr: 22016279	y

Citation Nr: A22007115	y
Citation Nr: 22015409	n
Citation Nr: 22005456	y
Citation Nr: A22007648	n
Citation Nr: A22004040	y
Citation Nr: 22003451	n
Citation Nr: 22021527	y
Citation Nr: 22005918	y
Citation Nr: A22005347	n
Citation Nr: 22005393	n
Citation Nr: 22005456	y
Citation Nr: 22002916	y
Citation Nr: A22003123	y
Citation Nr: 22015748	n
Citation Nr: 22000888	n
Citation Nr: 22018169	n
Citation Nr: 22005209	y
Citation Nr: 22018250	n
Citation Nr: 22003130	y
Citation Nr: A22001074	y
Citation Nr: A22001066	y
Citation Nr: A22000192	y
Citation Nr: A22004725	y
Citation Nr: 22007185	y
Citation Nr: 22013776	n
Citation Nr: 22017234	n
Citation Nr: 22007215	n

Citation Nr: 22017900	y
Citation Nr: A22004134	y
Citation Nr: A22004486	y
Citation Nr: 22018116	y
Citation Nr: 22014529	n
Citation Nr: 22011607	n
Citation Nr: 22012674	n
Citation Nr: 22012773	n
Citation Nr: A22000066	y
Citation Nr: 22020880	y
Citation Nr: 22024999	y
Citation Nr: 22014542	y
Citation Nr: 22003807	n
Citation Nr: 22020884	n
Citation Nr: 22023436	y
Citation Nr: A22000341	n
Citation Nr: 22002870	y
Citation Nr: A22000900	y
Citation Nr: 22023679	n
Citation Nr: A22001643	n
Citation Nr: 22018229	y
Citation Nr: 22008951	n
Citation Nr: 22023405	n
Citation Nr: 22002399	y
Citation Nr: 22009934	n
Citation Nr: 22015458	n
Citation Nr: 22013919	y

Citation Nr: 22009100	n
Citation Nr: 22024771	y
Citation Nr: 22016361	y
Citation Nr: 22005947	y
Citation Nr: 22012682	n
Citation Nr: 22019176	n
Citation Nr: A22002058	n
Citation Nr: 22000236	n
Citation Nr: A22006107	y
Citation Nr: 22001860	y
Citation Nr: 22002747	n
Citation Nr: A22001845	n
Citation Nr: 22020009	y
Citation Nr: 22001439	n
Citation Nr: A22005399	n
Citation Nr: 22022196	n
Citation Nr: 22012663	y
Citation Nr: 22019768	y
Citation Nr: 22024573	y
Citation Nr: A22002044	y
Citation Nr: 22023489	y
Citation Nr: 22006336	y
Citation Nr: 22016857	y
Citation Nr: A22004816	y

If VA decisions were accurate and reliable then it shouldn't be anything close to something like a coin-flip when denied sleep apnea secondary to PTSD claims go to the

BVA for appeal, right? Yet it is something like a coin flip. If the previous denials were correct, half of the denials shouldn't be getting overturned as though they were incorrect. However, this isn't a phenomenon exclusive to sleep apnea secondary to PTSD. Data related to all decisions made by BVA, for comparison, reflects a similar concern in general for all cases. You can interpret the results below in the context of all cases which go to the BVA. In fact, a large percentage of cases which had been denied become allowed later when they go to the BVA. If those earlier denials were appropriate and accurate, why would so many of those denials be overturned later at BVA? Hint: they probably shouldn't have been denied in the first place. While it is true that the Veteran may have obtained additional evidence such as a nexus letter and then approved, this also reflects that the assistance available to them or the opinions from the C&P examiner may have not been adequate.

A chart based on the BVA's 2021 report related to all cases-not just sleep apnea secondary to PTSD (see https://www.bva.va.gov/docs/Chairmans_Annual_Rpts/BVA2021AR.pdf)

Difference in Case Disposition Outcomes for Cases Upon Which a BVA Hearing Had Been Held

Hearing Venue	Allowed	Denied	Remand	Other	Total Cases
Central Office	32%	22%	42%	4%	1,742
Video Tele-Conference	30%	25%	41%	4%	17,771
Virtual	52%	10%	35%	**2%**	13,215

When not looking at remands, just claim allowances and denials, more of the cases were allowed than denied (despite previously having been denied potentially more than once at earlier phases in the process).

Another issue that can lead to decisions being overturned later is the system in place where poorly trained contractors with little expertise in the subject matter conduct examinations. The quality and training of contractors can be hit or miss. I worked with both VES and QTC in the past myself. However, the experience, training and quality of exams from contractors can vary. For example, one examination for sleep apnea may be conducted by a board certified physician who is a sleep medicine specialist, while another may be conducted by a physician, PA or NP with little or no substantial expertise relevant to sleep apnea or PTSD. However, this is also true of VA employees who may conduct exams. In fact, some

VA's have had providers with little experience or training in conducting disability exams do C&P exams in addition to their other duties (despite having little familiarity with the process or forensic work). In terms of contractors, per the VA's own OIG "contract exams are a significant investment, and VA has spent nearly $6.8 billion since fiscal year 2017. Some of the exams produced by vendors have not met contractual accuracy requirements. As a result, claims processors may have used inaccurate or insufficient medical evidence to decide veterans' claims. Therefore, it is vital for VBA to improve the governance and accountability of the program." The OIG found that the contractors QTC, VES and LHI "failed to consistently provide VBA with the accurate exams required by the contracts." The OIG notes that "ALL THREE VENDORS HAVE BEEN BELOW THE CONTRACT'S 92% ACCURACY REQUIREMENT SINCE AT LEAST 2017." Most errors–including a significant number that "had the potential to affect claims decisions–" aren't corrected before the claims processors decided the claims per the OIG. [*See: https://www.va.gov/oig/publications/report-summary.asp?id=5152*]

VA researchers have also identified contract exams as being plagued with errors. The VA researchers noted *"there are several possible explanations for the observed deficiencies in contract exams, including lack of supervision, more limited access to VA treatment records, and inadequate training and experience. An additional explanation is that, unlike exams by salaried VA staff, contractors are paid a flat fee for each exam which is a small fraction of the typical fees paid for forensic psychological evaluation in the community. Thus, there is a financial incentive to complete exams quickly, which would preclude careful record review, psychological testing, and detailed report preparation."* The authors go on to suggest that *"anecdotally, it is not uncommon for veterans seen by contractors needing to be reexamined, at times with requests for second and even third opinions to resolve "conflicting medical evidence" after a contract examiner rendered an opinion that contradicted those in the veteran's records or in previous C&P exams. Inefficiencies resulting from poor exams increase the workload for both examiners and VBA personnel and increase the costs for VA C&P operations overall"* [see Meisler, A. W., & Gianoli, M. O. (2022). The Department of Veterans Affairs disability examination program for PTSD: Critical analysis and strategies for remediation. Psychology, Public Policy, and Law].

CONCLUDING REMARKS

Thank you.

If you know a Veteran in need of a nexus letter for sleep apnea secondary to PTSD (or another psychological condition) or other issues, you can send them to NexusLetters.com. They can get Dr. Finnerty's information there as well as a list of other professionals who may be able to help on this or other issues. Dr. Finnerty also provides telehealth examinations for Veterans who may need a mental health diagnosis or are looking for a rating increase in their already service connected PTSD or other psychological condition. Dr Finnerty can also address other disability related issues such as evaluations focused on Social Security disability claims.

At nexusletters.com Veterans and others who are interested can also sign up for Dr. Finnerty's e-mail mailing list. Dr. Finnerty writes a very occasional e-mail newsletter with news about his practice related to nexus letters as well as general news related to VA disability claims in general. You can sign up at http://nexusletters.com/e-mail-newsletter-subscribe/

Please help other Veterans know whether they should read this book. Please rate this book on Amazon and

anywhere else you feel is relevant.

ADDENDUM: NEXUS-RELATED EXCERPTS FROM 51 DIFFERENT CASES APPROVED FOR SLEEP APNEA BY BVA

Dr. Finnerty reviewed 102 BVA cases related to sleep apnea secondary to PTSD from early 2022. The next 51 excerpts are quoted from the 2022 approval decisions used in Dr. Finnerty's analysis. These decisions helped him arrive at the conclusion that it is at least as likely as not that your previous denial for sleep apnea secondary to PTSD will be overturned, and your case approved, if BVA makes a decision on it. The remaining text in this book are quotations directly from decisions where Veterans were successful at obtaining benefits for sleep apnea after a BVA decision.

Citation Nr: A22007315

In conjunction with a VA PTSD examination, another opinion was provided by a VA examiner in July 2015. The examiner opined that it was less likely than not that the Veteran's sleep apnea was caused by his PTSD, as there are multiple medical problems that impact sleep apnea, such as obesity, smoking, alcohol use, genetics, physiology, and others. The examiner found there are no controlled, scientific studies documented that PTSD causes obstructive sleep apnea but there are multiple studies showing a correlation between sleep apnea and PTSD, but no causation had been established. The examiner did not address whether the Veteran's sleep apnea was aggravated by his service-connected PTSD.

Another private opinion is of record from August 2015. The examiner opined it is likely that the Veteran's sleep apnea is secondary to his PTSD, as his PTSD aggravates his sleep apnea. The examiner noted that a review of the medical and behavioral health literature supports a positive nexus between sleep apnea and PTSD and that, based on the examiner's education, training, and experience, it is at least as likely as not that his sleep apnea is certainly aggravated by his PTSD. As rationale for this opinion, the examiner stated that the chronic activation of stress hormones from PTSD is known to lead to a neural sensitization leading to upper airway dysfunction such as sleep apnea.

An additional private opinion is of record from March 2018. The examiner, who has been following the Veteran for his sleep apnea, opined it was more likely than not that the Veteran's PTSD is an aggravating factor in his sleep apnea. Like the August 2015 private examiner, the examiner noted that the stress hormones associated with PTSD can lead to upper airway dysfunction associated with sleep apnea. The examiner noted that there is established medical research establishes that PTSD aggravates sleep apnea and reviewed the Veteran's medical history. The examiner recorded the Veteran's contentions that his sleep apnea is made worse by his PTSD, as the Veteran's dreams leave him startled and paranoid and that the Veteran is highly sensitive to sounds and anything touching him, so he is prone to tear off his CPAP (continuous positive airway pressure) mask and experiences less restful, restorative sleep. The examiner concluded that, based on the medical literature and the Veteran's medical history, there is a relationship between the Veteran's sleep apnea and his PTSD based on aggravation.

The most recent VA examination is of record from March 2020. The examiner only addressed the question of direct service connection and opined that it was less likely than not that the Veteran's sleep apnea was incurred in, or caused by, his service, as the Veteran's service treatment records do not reflect any signs, symptoms, or a diagnosis of obstructive sleep apnea during service. The examiner did not address secondary service connection or the question of aggravation.

Citation Nr: 22014071

In this case, the evidence, taken together as a whole, reflects that the Veteran's service-connected PTSD caused his obstructive sleep apnea.

For example, in a July 2019 treatment record, the Veteran's private treatment provider (who specializes in pulmonary, sleep, and critical care medicine) physically examined the Veteran, provided a medical history of the Veteran's obstructive sleep apnea, indicated that the Veteran was currently being treated for his PTSD symptoms, and stated that the Veteran's obstructive sleep apnea is "as likely as not to be caused in part by PTSD".

Also, in May 2020 email correspondence, a Doctor of Philosophy, R.R. (who is a post-doctoral research fellow in the division of sleep and circadian disorder) stated that a medical article, titled Journal of Clinical Sleep Medicine, found a "strong link between PTSD and OSA." Specifically, R. Robbins indicated that the medical article shows that males who are 55 and older with PTSD were 83 percent more likely to have obstructive sleep apnea.

The Board finds that the July 2019 treatment provider's statement that the Veteran's obstructive sleep apnea is "as likely as not to be caused in part by PTSD" is highly probative as to whether the Veteran's obstructive sleep apnea was caused by his service-connected PTSD. To this extent, although the July 2019 physician did not provide a rationale following his statement, the July 2019 private treatment record reflects that the statement was based on a physical examination of the Veteran, his history of sleep apnea and PTSD, and the July 2019 treatment provider's medical expertise. To this extent, the July 2019 treatment provider specializes in sleep disorders. See Monzingo v. Shinseki, 26 Vet. App. 97, 106 (2012) (the fact that the rationale provided by an examiner "did not explicitly lay out the examiner's journey from the facts to a conclusion," did not render the examination inadequate); Acevedo v. Shinseki, 25 Vet. App. 286, 294 (2012) (medical reports must be read as a whole and in the context of the evidence of record).

While the May 2020 email correspondence may not specifically indicate that the Veteran's obstructive sleep apnea was caused by his service-connected PTSD, the May 2020 email correspondence is probative as to whether there is a relationship between obstructive sleep apnea and PTSD, as the Doctor of Philosophy, R.R., cited to a medical article which found that individuals (who are males and 55 and older-such as the Veteran) with PTSD are at a very high risk of developing obstructive sleep apnea. Also, the medical article was provided by a Doctor of Philosophy, R.R., who is a post-doctoral research fellow in the division of sleep and circadian disorder.

There is one VA negative opinion of record, dated in November 2018, that found that the Veteran's obstructive sleep apnea is less likely than not due to or the result of his PTSD. The November 2018 opinion is afforded no probative value, as the favorable evidence of record was not addressed or considered.

See Gabrielson v. Brown, 7 Vet. App. 36, 40 (1994) (the Board may not simply adopt a medical examiner's opinion that fails to discuss favorable evidence of record but must instead account for that favorable evidence with an adequate statement of reasons or bases).

In sum, the Board finds that the evidence weighs persuasively in favor of finding that the Veteran's obstructive sleep apnea was caused by his service-connected PTSD. See 38 U.S.C. § 5107(b); Lynch v. McDonough, No. 20-2067 (Fed. Cir. 2021). Accordingly, service connection for obstructive sleep apnea, as secondary to service-connected PTSD, is warranted.

Citation Nr: A22001989

The question then becomes whether a nexus, or relationship, between the Veteran's current disability and the Veteran's service-connected disability has been shown.

In a December 2019 report, L.B., MPAS, PA-C, opined that the Veteran's sleep apnea was more likely than not due to his PTSD. She indicated that she reviewed the Veteran's medical history, as well as the circumstances and events of his military service. She noted that the Veteran's poor sleep quality and excessive daytime fatigue began around the same time period as his PTSD. She also indicated that the Veteran gained weight after his PTSD diagnosis due to the Veteran's difficulties with even mundane tasks, such as exercise. She cited to several research studies showing that patients with PTSD are more likely to be diagnosed with sleep apnea than the general population because PTSD is associated with a fragmented sleep pattern of REM sleep, which in turn cause hypotonia of the muscles of the upper airway causing a functional obstruction of the upper airways. She also noted that chronic activation of stress hormones caused by PTSD "is well known to lead to a neural sensitization leading to upper airway dysfunction, and thus OSA." She noted a

2010 study documenting increased sleep apnea in combat Veterans with PTSD, which showed that 54 percent of combat Veteran's who underwent sleep studies were diagnosed with obstructive sleep apnea, compared with 20 percent of the general population. She also noted a 2015 study in the Journal of Clinical Sleep Medicine, which supported the 2010 study by demonstrating that of 159 Veterans screened, 69 percent were assessed as being at a high risk for obstructive sleep apnea. Finally, she cited to an ongoing study, the Millennium Cohort Study, which began in 2001 and involves more than 77,000 military service members, showing a link between PTSD and weight gain.

In a February 2020 letter, the Veteran's private physician, Dr. J.C., indicated that he reviewed L.B.'s report and that he concurred with her opinion that the Veteran's obstructive sleep apnea was more likely than not due to his service-connected PTSD.

The Veteran was afforded a VA examination in April 2020. The examiner opined that the Veteran's sleep apnea was less likely as not related to his service-connected PTSD. The examiner noted that the Veteran was not diagnosed with sleep apnea until 42 years post-service. The examiner also indicated that the studies cited in L.B.'s report do not prove a causal relationship. Specifically, the examiner noted that while medical studies have shown a "proven correlation between PTSD and OSA...a correlation does not establish a causal relationship."

The Board finds that the positive and negative opinions are nearly equal on the issue of whether the Veteran's currently diagnosed sleep apnea is causally related to his service-connected PTSD. In this regard, the VA examiner and the private examiner reviewed the claims file and interviewed the Veteran prior to rendering the opinions. Moreover, the opinions are supported by an adequate rationale and the other medical evidence of record. Accordingly, the Board finds that the evidence is nearly equal as to whether the Veteran's currently diagnosed sleep apnea is causally related to his service-connected PTSD. When the evidence for and against the claim is nearly equal, by law, the Board must resolve all reasonable doubt in favor of the claimant. Therefore, the Board finds that service connection for sleep apnea, as secondary to service-connected PTSD, is warranted. 38 U.S.C. 5107; 38 C.F.R. 3.102; Gilbert v. Derwinski, 1 Vet. App. 49, 54 (1990).

Citation Nr: 22015892

To establish service connection for a claimed disability on a secondary basis, there must be (1) medical evidence of a current disability; (2) a service-connected disability; and (3) medical evidence of a nexus between the service-connected disease or injury and the current disability. See Wallin v. West, 11 Vet. App. 509, 512 (1998).

The United States Court of Appeals for Veterans Claims (the Court) has held that "[g]enerally, an attempt to establish a medical nexus to a disease or injury solely by generic information in a medical journal or treatise is too general and inconclusive." Mattern v. West, 12 Vet. App. 222, 228 (1999) (citing Sacks v. West, 11 Vet. App. 314, 317 (1998)). The Court has, however, also held that medical treatise evidence "standing alone, discusses generic relationships with a degree of certainty such that, under the facts of a specific case, there is at least plausible causality based upon objective facts rather than on an unsubstantiated lay medical opinion." Wallin v. West, 11 Vet. App. 509, 514 (1998) (citing Sacks, 11 Vet. App. at 317). The United States Court of Appeals for Federal Circuit (the Federal Circuit) held that "[a] veteran with a competent medical diagnosis of a current disorder may invoke an accepted medical treatise in order to establish the required nexus; in an appropriate case it should not be necessary to obtain the services of medical personnel to show how the treatise applies to his [or her] case." Hensley v. West, 212 F.3d 1255, 1265 (2000).

Analysis

Various VA examination reports and VA treatment records reveal a diagnosis of obstructive sleep apnea. Therefore, Wallin element (1), current disability, is established.

Service connection is in effect for PTSD. Thus, Wallin element (2), service-connected disability, is shown.

Turning to medical nexus, there is conflicting medical evidence.

A 2018 VA study titled Obstructive Sleep Apnea in Posttraumatic Stress Disorder Comorbid with Mood Disorder: Significantly Higher Incidence than in Either Diagnosis Alone showed a high prevalence of obstructive sleep apnea in psychiatric patients, particularly in those with PTSD and major depressive disorder and less so with bipolar disorder. The study also showed that there is a statistically significant increase in the incidence of obstructive sleep apnea in male veterans with either bipolar disorder with comorbid PTSD or major depressive disorder with comorbid PTSD.

In a February 2019 written brief presentation, the representative cited an article from the National Institutes of Health (NIH) showing that there may be an increased prevalence of obstructive sleep apnea in individuals with major depressive disorder and in individuals with PTSD.

A November 2019 VA PTSD examination report reveals that the examiner opined that it is less likely than not that the obstructive sleep apnea was proximately due to the service-connected PTSD. The examiner stated that PTSD does not cause obstructive sleep apnea. The examiner added that while obstructive sleep apnea can be co-morbid with PTSD, obstructive sleep apnea is not induced or caused by PTSD.

A November 2019 VA sleep apnea examination report reflects that the examiner opined that it is less likely than not that the sleep apnea is due to or the result of the PTSD. The examiner stated that the current medical literature remains silent for any mechanism by which PTSD, a psychiatric disorder, may cause obstructive sleep apnea, an anatomically based disorder. The examiner noted that the NIH study cited by the representative does not establish direct cause and effect between PTSD and obstructive sleep apnea.

In a February 2021 addendum to the November 2019 VA sleep apnea examination report, the November 2019 examiner again opined that it is less likely than not that the sleep apnea is due to or the result of the PTSD. The examiner reiterated that current medical literature remains silent for any mechanism by which PTSD, a psychiatric disorder, may cause obstructive sleep apnea. The examiner indicated that obstructive sleep apnea is caused by the muscles in the throat relaxing, which results in the airway being narrowed or closed and a momentary cut off of breathing.

In an April 2021 written brief presentation, the representative cited "The Connection Between Sleep Apnea and PTSD", which was published at the Sleep Foundation's website in February 2021. The representative stated that the article notes that whereas only 17 to 22 percent of the general population have sleep apnea, 12 to 90 percent of people with PTSD have sleep apnea. The representative added that the article states that 69 percent of Vietnam veterans with PTSD show indications of PTSD. The Board notes that the Veteran served in the Republic of Vietnam.

In a June 2021 addendum to the November 2019 VA sleep

apnea examination report, the November 2019 examiner again opined that it is less likely than not that the sleep apnea is proximately due to the PTSD. The examiner noted that study published by the Sleep Foundation shows an increased risk of obstructive sleep apnea in veterans with PTSD but does not find causation. The examiner indicated that the NIH study finds that there is an elevated risk of obstructive sleep apnea with PTSD but no causation.

In a November 2011 medical opinion, a VA doctor opined that it is less likely than not that the sleep apnea is proximately due to the PTSD. The clinician stated that while the current literature suggests that PTSD may play some role in obstructive sleep apnea, this conclusion is not definitive and that more research is needed.

The physician cited a study of Australian Vietnam veterans with and without PTSD that shows no difference across all polysomnography parameters, include the diagnoses and severity of obstructive sleep apnea and periodic limb movements of sleep. The clinician added that this study reveals that Vietnam veterans with PTSD demonstrated an increased perception of sleep disturbances.

The doctor discussed the study from the Sleep Foundation. The physician noted that the source study divides patients with obstructive sleep apnea with PTSD and without PTSD and that there was less adherence to use of a continuous positive airway pressure (CPAP) machine with PTSD patients compared to patients without PTSD. The clinician stated that the study does not indicate a stronger association and that it discusses less compliance with treatment. The doctor added that several statements in the article were not consistent with their sources.

The doctor quoted a 2018 entry at the VA website "It is possible that PTSD and chronic arousal are related to OSA [obstructive sleep apnea] bidirectionally, as research has yet to definitely determine temporality." The physician noted that entry states that it is possible that the two disorders are related but that research has yet to definitely determine temporality.

Given that the VA doctor who prepared the November 2021 medical opinion noted the possibility of a relationship between PTSD and obstructive sleep apnea and stated that the current literature suggests that PTSD may play some role in obstructive sleep apnea, the evidence is in equipoise as to whether the obstructive sleep apnea was caused by PTSD. Wallin element (3), medical nexus, is established. Therefore, service connection for obstructive sleep apnea by means of causation is in order. 38 U.S.C. §§ 1110, 5107.

As the Board is granted service connection for obstructive sleep apnea as secondary to PTSD via causation, the Board does not have to address whether the sleep apnea began in service, whether the sleep apnea was aggravated by PTSD, and whether the sleep apnea is related to the service-connected lumbar spine disability and type II diabetes mellitus.

Citation Nr: A22002833

Entitlement to service connection for sleep apnea, claimed as secondary to service-connected adjustment disorder with PTSD.

The Veteran has advanced the very narrow theory of entitlement to service connection for sleep apnea as secondary to his service-connected PTSD. Robinson v. Shinseki, 557 F.3d 1355, 1361 (2008). In this regard, service connection may be established on a secondary basis for a disability which is proximately due to or the result of service-connected disease or injury. 38 U.S.C. §§ 1110, 1131; 38 C.F.R. § 3.310(a). Establishing service connection on a secondary basis requires evidence sufficient to show (1) that a current disability exists and (2) that the current disability was either

(a) proximately caused by or (b) proximately aggravated by a service-connected disability. Allen v. Brown, 7 Vet. App. 439, 448 (1995) (en banc). Further, service connection may not be awarded on the basis of aggravation without establishing a pre-aggravation baseline level of disability and comparing it to the current level of disability. 38 C.F.R. § 3.310(b).

In the December 2019 rating decision, the AOJ favorably found that the Veteran has a current diagnosis of sleep apnea as demonstrated by his VA treatment records, and is service-connected for adjustment disorder with PTSD. Consequently, the remaining inquiry is whether the Veteran's sleep apnea is caused or aggravated by his service-connected adjustment disorder with PTSD.

In this regard, in September 2019, L.B., a board-certified physician assistant, opined that the Veteran's sleep apnea was more likely than not proximately due to or the result of his service-connected PTSD. In support thereof, she reported that she reviewed the Veteran's medical history and noted that: (1) the Veteran attested that his symptoms of PTSD began while in service; (2) he indicated that his poor sleep quality and excessive daytime fatigue began around the same period; (3) he denied a history of sleep apnea or other sleep disturbances prior to his enlistment; and (4) he was eventually diagnosed with obstructive sleep apnea through a sleep study in 2014.

Specifically, L.B. explained that a study conducted at the Walter Reed Medical Center, published in 2010, documented increased sleep apnea in combat veterans with PTSD. She further explained that a study published in the Journal of Clinical Sleep Medicine in 2015 supported the aforementioned findings as such demonstrated that, of 159 OEF/OIF/OND veterans screened, 69.2 percent were assessed as being at risk for obstructive sleep apnea; PTSD symptom severity increased the risk of screening positive for obstructive sleep apnea; and veterans with PTSD screened as high risk for obstructive sleep apnea at much higher rates than those seen in community studies and may not show all the classic predictors of obstructive sleep apnea (i.e., older and higher BMI). Thus, L.B. concluded that medical research studies had shown that patients with PTSD were more likely to be diagnosed with obstructive sleep apnea than the general population; PTSD was associated with a fragmented pattern of REM sleep; abnormalities of REM sleep caused hypotonia of the muscles in the upper airway, which created a functional obstruction of the upper airways, resulting in obstructive sleep apnea; and chronic activation of stress hormones caused by PTSD was well known to led to a neural sensitization leading to upper airway dysfunction, and thus obstructive sleep apnea.

Conversely, in October 2019, a VA examiner, who is an advanced practice registered nurse, reviewed the record, interviewed the Veteran, and conducted an examination, and opined that it was less likely than not that the Veteran's sleep apnea was proximately due to or the result of his service-connected PTSD. As rationale for the opinion, she indicated that, according to UpToDate, obstructive sleep apnea was the most common sleep-related breathing disorder; obstructive sleep apnea was most common among older males, but it could also affect women and children; and risk factors for sleep apnea were: older age, male gender, obesity, craniofacial and upper airway abnormalities, smoking, family history of snoring or obstructive sleep apnea, and nasal congestion. The examiner further indicated that the prevalence of obstructive sleep apnea was increased in patients with a variety of medical conditions: obesity, hypoventilation syndrome, congestive heart failure, hypertension, end stage renal disease, diabetes mellitus, type II, chronic lung disease, stroke and transient ischemic attacks, pregnancy, acromegaly, hypothyroidism, polycystic ovary syndrome, Parkinson's disease, and floppy eyelid syndrome. Additionally, she noted that the following medical conditions may have an increased association with obstructive sleep apnea: fibromyalgia, gastroesophageal reflux disease, secondary polycythemia, and Down's syndrome. However, whether there was an increased prevalence of obstructive sleep apnea in PTSD was unclear at such time.

As both L.B. and the October 2019 VA examiner are medical professionals, considered all relevant evidence, and offered a rationale for their opinions, their opinions are entitled to equal probative weight. Consequently, the Board resolves all doubt in the Veteran's favor and finds that his currently diagnosed sleep apnea is proximately due to his service-connected PTSD. Therefore, service connection for such disorder is warranted. 38 U.S.C. § 5107; 38 C.F.R. § 3.102.

Citation Nr: 22009908

When there is an approximate balance of positive and negative evidence regarding any issue material to the determination of a matter, the Secretary shall give the benefit of the doubt to the claimant. 38 U.S.C. § 7105; 38 C.F.R. §§ 3.102, 4.3. When a claimant seeks benefits and the evidence is in relative equipoise, the claimant prevails. See Gilbert v. Derwinski, 1 Vet. App. 49, 53-54 (1990). The preponderance of the evidence must be against the claim for benefits to be denied. See Alemany v. Brown, 9 Vet. App. 518 (1996).

Entitlement to service connection for OSA on a secondary basis.

The Veteran contends that his currently diagnosed obstructive sleep apnea had onset during service. Alternatively, the Veteran contends that service connection for obstructive sleep apnea is warranted on a secondary basis as due to his service-connected PTSD, diabetes mellitus, hypertension, and/or IHD.

As mentioned above, service connection may be established on a secondary basis for a disability that is proximately due to or the result of a service-connected disease or injury. See 38 C.F.R. § 3.310(a); Harder v. Brown, 5 Vet. App. 183, 187 (1993). Additional disability resulting from the aggravation of a nonservice-connected condition by a service-connected condition is also compensable under 38 C.F.R. § 3.310 (a). See Allen v. Brown, 7 Vet. App. 439, 448 (1995).

At his May 2017 Board hearing, the Veteran testified that he believes that his OSA began in the 1970s during service or shortly after as his wife at the time would often wake him up because she thought he had stopped breathing. In a statement submitted in August 2008, the Veteran stated that as far back as the 1970's he has always complained of being tired and did not feel rested after sleeping. See also September 2008 Statement.

The Veteran's service treatment records do not show any treatments, complaints, or diagnosis for obstructive sleep apnea. The Veteran's private treatment records show that he was first diagnosed with obstructive sleep apnea in 2003 approximately sixteen years after his separation from active military service. Moderate obstructive sleep apnea was confirmed in an October 2019 sleep study.

The Veteran was afforded a VA examination in May 2018. The examiner reviewed the record and noted that the Veteran's sleep apnea was diagnosed in 2003 by a sleep study. The examiner opined that the Veteran's sleep apnea was less likely than not incurred in or caused by an in-service injury, event, or illness.

The examiner opined that the Veteran's sleep apnea was not caused by the Veteran's hypertension because, as a general matter, sleep apnea was not caused by hypertension. The examiner stated that the most common cause of obstructive sleep apnea is excess of weight and that the Veteran at the of his sleep study was obese, has an extensive history of smoking which has likely been a contributing factor for changes in respiratory tree contributing to development of sleep apnea. He also stated that there is no medical evidence to support sleep apnea was present or diagnosed during service and that the lay statements provided by the Veteran and his wife were inconsistent with service treatment records. Regarding the article submitted by the Veteran from the Journal of Clinical Sleep Medicine: Obstructive Sleep Apnea and Post-Traumatic Stress Disorder among OEF/OIF/OND Veterans, the examiner "reviewed the study, and noted the sample size was too small to be generalizable (only 195 veterans were included in study) and noted the researchers recommendations were for validation of OSA screening measures with this population as well as longitudinal studies of OSA and PTSD to further understand the interplay between the two disorders and trajectories of clinical interventions. Further research studies using appropriate sample sizes as well as reliable and validated measures need to be conducted. Veteran was not deployed to The Gulf and was not exposed to burn pits, sandstorms, or environmental toxins particular to The Gulf."

Additionally, the examiner opined that the Veteran sleep apnea is not proximately due to his service-connected PTSD as "OSA and PSTD can co-exist but there is no compelling medical evidence or research to show a cause-and-effect relationship." Regarding aggravation, the examiner opined that the Veteran's OSA is not aggravated by the Veteran's service-connected PTSD, HIS or diabetes. For the PTSD, the examiner's rationale was that "sleep apnea causes an individual to awaken before the deepest level of REM sleep is reached, which is when dreams/nightmares (associated with PTSD) occur, and therefore, OSA is considered to actually prevent or suppress the occurrence of nightmares in the individual with PTSD. Veteran's sleep apnea is untreated as veteran declines to use CPAP therapy as ordered, so his sleep apnea symptoms are likely more significant than individuals who comply with prescribed treatment modalities. In regard to the service-connected IHD and diabetes the examiner simply stated as rationale that "there is no cause-and-effect relationship."

In an April 2021 VA opinion report, the examiner provided negative opinions with regard to causation for nearly all of the Veteran's service-connected disabilities. As the Veteran's contention have been limited to PTSD, diabetes, hypertension and IHD, the Board will address the examiner's opinions for these disabilities only. On IHD, the examiner reasoned that "while there is a well-known correlation between coronary artery disease and OSA, CAD is not the cause of OSA. The medical literature supports OSA as a risk factor for cardiovascular disease." The examiner stated that hypertension "is not a known cause of obstructive sleep apnea. In fact, in certain instances, OSA is actually a cause of secondary hypertension, not the reverse." On diabetes, the examiner stated that according to the American Diabetes Association website "...OSA has been shown to increase the risk and severity of type 2 diabetes independent of age and obesity. This is notable because age and obesity are risk factors for both OSA and type 2 diabetes." The bulk of the medical literature does not support the opinion that DMII is a cause of obstructive sleep apnea. Regarding PTSD, the examiner noted "[h]igh comorbidity rates suggest the importance of assessment for obstructive sleep apnea among patients with PTSD. A 2015 systematic review epidemiologic studies found obstructive sleep apnea to have the highest prevalence in patients with PTSD compared with other psychiatric disorders found that OSA prevalence was higher among people with PTSD and depression. Two population-based studies found prevalence rates of 46.4 and 50 percent in patients with sleep apnea. A review of 11 studies using a high-quality sleep measures found 63 percent of patients with PTSD had sleep disordered breathing. OSA and PTSD likely have shared pathophysiology with hypothalamic-pituitary-adrenal axis activation, sympathetic nervous symptom activation, brain changes in common areas hippocampus, amygdala, prefrontal cortex, sleep fragmentation, changes in REM, and microarousals." Citing Sareen, Stein, & Friedman (Up To Date, 2020) The examiner added that the Veteran's BMI on day of exam was 31.9 and neck circumference was 17.5. When he was diagnosed in 2003, BMI was 32 with a neck size of 17.5. Shared pathology does not create a proximal or causal relationship between PTSD and OSA. Although there are multiple studies showing a connection between the two diagnoses, the bulk of the medical literature does not show a definitive proximate or causative relationship between PTSD and OSA.

In a letter from July 2019, the Veteran's private doctor opined that the Veteran's sleep apnea is related to his military service. He reasoned that the Veteran's sleep apnea is severe enough to cause him to wake multiple times during the night and it has, over an extended period of time, caused him to have very erratic and non-restful sleep. All of the above have worsen his PTSD and is creating a vicious cycle whereby his PTSD exacerbates his sleep apnea, and his sleep apnea exacerbates his PTSD. He added that PTSD directly causes sleep apnea by negatively impacting the normal neurohumoral feedback mechanism within the central nervous system. It has been clearly demonstrated that heightened arousal disorders such as PTSD cause abnormal catecholamine metabolism and abnormal serotonin metabolism within the brain. Both of these molecules are critically important to normal sleep cycles and the disruption of their normal metabolism directly causes sleep apnea. Additionally, Type II Diabetes Mellitus -with its associated metabolic syndrome, over-secretion of insulin, and associated autoimmune phenomena- directly affects sleep in a negative matter and further exacerbates the sleep apnea caused by PTSD.

As the April 2021 examiner failed to address the question of aggravation, in October 2021, the Board remanded the issue on appeal to obtain an addendum opinion on the matter. In a November 2021 addendum medical opinion, the VA examiner opined that it is less likely than not that the Veteran's sleep apnea was aggravated beyond its natural progression by his PTSD, diabetes, IHD and/ or hypertension. The provided rationale is that there is no pathophysiologic mechanism for IHD, diabetes mellitus 2 and hypertension to cause or aggravate OSA.

In an April 2021 statement, the Veteran's wife reported that she has been married to the Veteran for 24 years and that for as long as they have been married the Veteran has had abnormal snoring and sleep activity and that he would stopped breathing between his snores, falls asleep at inappropriate times, while sitting on his chair, at his desk or at the dinner table. Also, that he uses a CPAP machine since 2019.

The Board notes that VA medical opinion on the etiology of the current OSA offered in May 2018 failed to consider whether the Veteran's currently diagnosed OSA was caused or aggravated by service-connected disabilities, other than PTSD, the Board finds it of limited value and less probative in the adjudication of this claim. Barr v. Nicholson, 21 Vet. App. 303, 312 (2007). While the April 2021 examiner cited studies that found obstructive sleep apnea to have the highest prevalence in patients with PTSD compared with other psychiatric disorders found that OSA prevalence was higher among people with PTSD and depression, he rendered a negative opinion because the bulk of the medical literature does not show a definitive proximate or causative relationship between PTSD and OSA and focused his opinion on the Veteran's neck size and BMI. While the November 2021 opinion did consider aggravation, it was merely to state that there is no pathophysiologic mechanism for IHD, diabetes mellitus 2 and hypertension to cause or aggravate OSA. That opinion does not discuss the multiple available medical studies or discuss what type of testing might be necessary to assess the question on appeal.

After careful consideration, the Board finds that the July 2019 opinion is most persuasive in this matter because it provides a sound basis upon which to base the decision on the issue adjudicated here. The opinion also considered the pertinent evidence of record, to include the Veteran's medical history, and provided a reasoned rationale which discussed the multiple available medical studies that are available which discuss possible aggravation of sleep apnea by PTSD.

In sum, the Board finds the July 2019 positive opinion more persuasive than the negative evidence of record. At the very least, it brings the evidence into relative equipoise as to whether or not the Veteran's sleep apnea has been caused or aggravated beyond natural progression by his PTSD.

When the evidence is in relative equipoise, the claimant prevails. See Gilbert v. Derwinski, 1 Vet. App. 49, 55 (1990). Since the July 2019 examiner, indicated PTSD both likely contributed to the development of and aggravates the Veteran's sleep apnea, the Board resolves reasonable doubt in the Veteran's favor in this regard and finds service connection is warranted for sleep apnea on a secondary basis based on a theory of causation without any consideration of a baseline level of disability prior to any potential aggravation. See 38 U.S.C. § 5107(b); 38 C.F.R. § 3.102. Accordingly, the claim is granted.

Citation Nr: 22015892

Turning to medical nexus, there is conflicting medical evidence.

A 2018 VA study titled Obstructive Sleep Apnea in

Posttraumatic Stress Disorder Comorbid with Mood Disorder: Significantly Higher Incidence than in Either Diagnosis Alone showed a high prevalence of obstructive sleep apnea in psychiatric patients, particularly in those with PTSD and major depressive disorder and less so with bipolar disorder. The study also showed that there is a statistically significant increase in the incidence of obstructive sleep apnea in male veterans with either bipolar disorder with comorbid PTSD or major depressive disorder with comorbid PTSD.

In a February 2019 written brief presentation, the representative cited an article from the National Institutes of Health (NIH) showing that there may be an increased prevalence of obstructive sleep apnea in individuals with major depressive disorder and in individuals with PTSD.

A November 2019 VA PTSD examination report reveals that the examiner opined that it is less likely than not that the obstructive sleep apnea was proximately due to the service-connected PTSD. The examiner stated that PTSD does not cause obstructive sleep apnea. The examiner added that while obstructive sleep apnea can be co-morbid with PTSD, obstructive sleep apnea is not induced or caused by PTSD.

A November 2019 VA sleep apnea examination report reflects that the examiner opined that it is less likely than not that the sleep apnea is due to or the result of the PTSD. The examiner stated that the current medical literature remains silent for any mechanism by which PTSD, a psychiatric disorder, may cause obstructive sleep apnea, an anatomically based disorder. The examiner noted that the NIH study cited by the representative does not establish direct cause and effect between PTSD and obstructive sleep apnea.

In a February 2021 addendum to the November 2019 VA sleep apnea examination report, the November 2019 examiner again opined that it is less likely than not that the sleep apnea is due to or the result of the PTSD. The examiner reiterated that current medical literature remains silent for any mechanism by which PTSD, a psychiatric disorder, may cause obstructive sleep apnea. The examiner indicated that obstructive sleep apnea is caused by the muscles in the throat relaxing, which results in the airway being narrowed or closed and a momentary cut off of breathing.

In an April 2021 written brief presentation, the representative cited "The Connection Between Sleep Apnea and PTSD", which was published at the Sleep Foundation's website in February 2021. The representative stated that the article notes that whereas only 17 to 22 percent of the general population have sleep apnea, 12 to 90 percent of people with PTSD have sleep apnea. The representative added that the article states that 69 percent of Vietnam veterans with PTSD show indications of PTSD. The Board notes that the Veteran served in the Republic of Vietnam.

In a June 2021 addendum to the November 2019 VA sleep apnea examination report, the November 2019 examiner again opined that it is less likely than not that the sleep apnea is proximately due to the PTSD. The examiner noted that study published by the Sleep Foundation shows an increased risk of obstructive sleep apnea in veterans with PTSD but does not find causation. The examiner indicated that the NIH study finds that there is an elevated risk of obstructive sleep apnea with PTSD but no causation.

In a November 2011 medical opinion, a VA doctor opined that it is less likely than not that the sleep apnea is proximately due to the PTSD. The clinician stated that while the current literature suggests that PTSD may play some role in obstructive sleep apnea, this conclusion is not definitive and that more research is needed.

The physician cited a study of Australian Vietnam veterans

with and without PTSD that shows no difference across all polysomnography parameters, include the diagnoses and severity of obstructive sleep apnea and periodic limb movements of sleep. The clinician added that this study reveals that Vietnam veterans with PTSD demonstrated an increased perception of sleep disturbances.

The doctor discussed the study from the Sleep Foundation. The physician noted that the source study divides patients with obstructive sleep apnea with PTSD and without PTSD and that there was less adherence to use of a continuous positive airway pressure (CPAP) machine with PTSD patients compared to patients without PTSD. The clinician stated that the study does not indicate a stronger association and that it discusses less compliance with treatment. The doctor added that several statements in the article were not consistent with their sources.

The doctor quoted a 2018 entry at the VA website "It is possible that PTSD and chronic arousal are related to OSA [obstructive sleep apnea] bidirectionally, as research has yet to definitely determine temporality." The physician noted that entry states that it is possible that the two disorders are related but that research has yet to definitely determine temporality.

Given that the VA doctor who prepared the November 2021 medical opinion noted the possibility of a relationship between PTSD and obstructive sleep apnea and stated that the current literature suggests that PTSD may play some role in obstructive sleep apnea, the evidence is in equipoise as to whether the obstructive sleep apnea was caused by PTSD. Wallin element (3), medical nexus, is established. Therefore, service connection for obstructive sleep apnea by means of causation is in order. 38 U.S.C. §§ 1110, 5107.

As the Board is granted service connection for obstructive sleep apnea as secondary to PTSD via causation, the Board does not have to address whether the sleep apnea began in service, whether the sleep apnea was aggravated by PTSD, and whether the sleep apnea is related to the service-connected lumbar spine disability and type II diabetes mellitus.

Citation Nr: 22016279

Sleep Apnea, as secondary to PTSD

The Veteran contends that his current disability of sleep apnea is related to his service-connected PTSD, including weight gain caused by the medications prescribed for his PTSD.

The Veteran is able to establish that he has a current disability of sleep apnea as reflected in the VA treatment records and the July 2019 VA examination. The Veteran's condition was diagnosed in a January 2018 sleep study. The Veteran is also service connected for PTSD. The remaining question is thus whether the Veteran's sleep apnea is caused by or aggravated by his service-connected PTSD.

The July 2019 VA examiner concluded that the Veteran's sleep apnea was less likely than not related to his PTSD because it was a physical condition unrelated to the mental condition. The examiner acknowledged studies that suggest a connection between sleep apnea and PTSD, but concluded that such a connection was "not true in 50% of the times." The Board finds this opinion inadequate because it does not address the contention that the medication the Veteran takes for PTSD caused him to gain weight, which in turn caused his sleep apnea. Moreover, the examiner did not offer an adequate rationale for its rejection of the studies acknowledging a connection between sleep apnea and PTSD.

The Veteran submitted positive nexus opinions from two VA treating physicians. The first, in April 2018, explained that the Veteran's medication for PTSD contributed to his weight gain, which in turn caused his sleep apnea. An August

2018 letter from another treating VA physician stated that the Veteran's sleep apnea was more likely than not caused by and exacerbated by his PTSD. The physician pointed to the existence of numerous studies documenting a relationship between sleep apnea and PTSD and explained that sleep apnea and PTSD share several commonalities. The physician also noted that PTSD disrupts the serotonergic system, which has a central role in the regulation of sleep/wakefulness and upper airway muscle tone during sleep.

The Board finds the opinions of the VA treating physicians entitled to probative weight. The April 2018 opinion is supported by the evidence in the medical records, which reflect that the Veteran is prescribed medication for PTSD and gained significant weight since 2015. The lay statements and testimony by the Veteran and his wife also described the Veteran's depression, lethargy and overeating related to his PTSD and medications. The Board notes that the United States Court of Appeals for Veterans Claims (CAVC) has held that obesity can serve as an "intermediate step" in a causal chain for service connection. Walsh v. Wilkie, 32 Vet. App. 300 (2020). According to CAVC, service connection may be granted on a secondary basis where the claimed disability would not have occurred but for obesity caused or aggravated by a service-connected disability. Id.

The August 2018 opinion is accompanied by an adequate rationale for the connection between the Veteran's sleep apnea and PTSD, with reference to relevant medical literature. See Stefl v. Nicholson, 21 Vet. App. 120, 124 (2007).

Based on the foregoing, the weight of the evidence supports a finding that the Veteran's sleep apnea is caused by his PTSD. Accordingly, the claim for service connection, as secondary to PTSD, is granted.

Citation Nr: A22007115

Service connection may be granted for disability resulting from disease or injury incurred in or aggravated by active service. 38 U.S.C. §§ 1131, 5107; 38 C.F.R. § 3.303. The three-element test for service connection requires evidence of: (1) a current disability; (2) in-service incurrence or aggravation of a disease or injury; and (3) a causal relationship between the current disability and the in-service disease or injury. Shedden v. Principi, 381 F.3d 1163, 1166 -67 (Fed. Cir. 2004).

Service connection may be granted for a disability that is proximately due to, or aggravated by, service-connected disease or injury. 38 C.F.R. § 3.310.

Entitlement to service connection for sleep disorders, to include insomnia and obstructive sleep apnea is granted.

The Veteran contends that his sleep apnea is secondary to his service-connected posttraumatic stress disorder (PTSD). He also contends that sleep apnea is directly related to his in-service exposure to burn pits.

The Board concludes that the Veteran has a current disability that is related to in-service exposure to burn pits. 38 U.S.C. §§ 1110, 1131, 5107(b); Holton v. Shinseki, 557 F.3d 1363, 1366 (Fed. Cir. 2009); 38 C.F.R. § 3.303(a).

During the course of the appeal, the AOJ issued favorable findings establishing that the Veteran had in-service exposure to burn pits and that he is currently diagnosed with sleep apnea.

The Veteran's VA Form DD 214 shows he served in Iraq from June 2006 to June 2007. Service treatment records indicate that the Veteran was seen with complaints of insomnia, secondary to environmental disturbances in October and November 2006; he was prescribed Ambien.

After service, the Veteran continued to endorse sleep problems and was given a trial use of trazodone in May 2009. While obstructive sleep apnea was diagnosed in February 2010, VA treatment records also show that he was still using trazodone in May 2010. The Veteran's mental health notes regularly reported insomnia as one of his medical problems. VA treatment records continue to show the Veteran's use of trazodone in May 2017 through April 2020.

The Veteran testified at his December 2021 hearing before the Board that after he returned from his deployment to Iraq, his wife of 47 years began informing him that he stopped breathing in his sleep.

A December 2018 VA examination report shows the Veteran has a current diagnosis of obstructive sleep apnea. The question before the Board is whether this current is related to service and/or to the Veteran's service-connected PTSD, as he asserts. On these questions, there are competent opinions in favor of and against the claim.

The evidence against the claim includes December 2018, September 2019, and June 2020 VA opinions.

The December 2018 VA examiner opined that the Veteran's obstructive sleep apnea was less likely as not proximately due to or aggravated by his service-connected PTSD. The examiner explained how obstructive sleep apnea was caused by an anatomic process and therefore "in no way related directly nor indirectly" to PTSD because it "would not result in this type of pathology." The examiner furthered that "as OSA is not anatomically related to PTSD, there is also no causality for an aggravation of OSA by PTSD."

A September 2019 VA examiner also provided an unfavorable nexus opinion regarding whether the Veteran's sleep apnea is related to his military service and environmental exposures therein. In providing the rationale, the examiner acknowledged the Veteran's in-service treatment for insomnia but explained that the medical literature does not support finding that insomnia is the cause of obstructive sleep apnea. The examiner explained, in detail, that the pathophysiology and developmental course of comorbid OSA and insomnia is not clearly understood. The examiner also discussed pertinent theoretical models as found in relevant medical literature to support the nexus opinion provided.

The June 2020 examiner addressed the Veteran's assertion that his sleep apnea is directly related to his in-service exposure to burn pits and also addressed whether sleep apnea is proximately caused by service-connected PTSD. In providing the unfavorable nexus opinions, the examiner reasoned that there is no known causal relationship between burn pit exposure and obstructive sleep apnea, noting that the pathophysiology of obstructive sleep apnea explained why PTSD and burn pit exposure "will not cause OSA." Additionally, the examiner noted that the Veteran's gender (male) and weight (obese) were "major risk factors for development in sleep apnea" and thus more likely the cause rather than PTSD and burn pit exposure.

The evidence in favor of the claim is a February 2019 VA contract examiner's opinion.

The February 2019 VA contract examiner opined that the Veteran's sleep apnea was at least as likely as not incurred in or caused by in-service environmental exposures. The examiner explained that the Veteran was exposed to open burn pits in Iraq and while in Iraq, he saw a military provider reporting shortness of breath related to the smoke exposure. Following his deployment in Iraq, in April 2009, the Veteran reported to VA mental health, that he had difficulty with sleeping. The examiner also noted the Veteran reported that his sleeping greatly decreased following his exposure to burn pits.

Of these competent medical opinions, the Board finds the

most probative are in relative equipoise regarding whether the Veteran's current obstructive sleep apnea is at least as likely as not related to service.

The February 2019 opinion and the June 2020 opinion (as it relates to direct service connection only) are both competent and persuasive on the question of whether the Veteran's sleep apnea is due to military service and burn pit exposure therein. Both examiners reviewed the pertinent clinical evidence, and the Veteran's reported symptoms of sleep problems/difficulty during service and thereafter, and offered unequivocal opinions that were supported by cogent rationale. Neither opinion outweighs the other in this regard. In short, the favorable February 2019 and unfavorable June 2020 opinions are in equipoise as it pertains to direct service connection.

In contrast, the September 2019 opinion addressed whether sleep apnea is related to active service, but did not address the specific contention regarding the claimed impact from the Veteran's burn pit exposures. Rather, it addresses whether the insomnia noted in service led to the current sleep apnea. For this reason, this opinion is of diminished probative weight because it is not fully comprehensive and does not provide the Board with the necessary information to render a fully-informed decision. See Nieves-Rodriguez v. Peake, 22 Vet. App. 295 (2008).

Finally, the December 2018 opinion only addresses the question of a causal relationship between sleep apnea and PTSD (i.e., secondary service connection), but not whether the Veteran's exposure to burn pits caused sleep apnea. Hence, it is not probative regarding direct service connection. The June 2020 nexus opinion - as it pertained to secondary service connection only- is flawed in that the examiner did not address whether the Veteran's service-connected PTSD had aggravated his sleep apnea. It only addressed proximate causation between service-connected PTSD and sleep apnea.

To that limited extent, the opinion is rejected. See 38 C.F.R. §
3.310 (b); El-Amin v. Shinseki, 26 Vet. App. 136, 140 (2013).

In sum, the competent and persuasive medical opinions
regarding a causal nexus between the Veteran's military
service and sleep apnea is at least in equipoise. Therefore, after
resolving all doubt in favor of the Veteran, service connection
for obstructive sleep apnea is warranted. 38 U.S.C. § 5107; 38
C.F.R. § 3.102.

Citation Nr: 22005456

By way of background, the Veteran reported in an April
2012 statement that he used food to cope with his stress
and anxiety, which led to problems with sleep apnea. In his
December 2013 Notice of Disagreement, the Veteran asserted
that the psychotropic medications he was prescribed for his
PTSD caused weight gain which caused sleep apnea. The Board
notes that, while obesity cannot be service-connected on a
direct basis, and obesity cannot qualify as an in-service event
for service connection purposes, obesity may indeed serve as
an "intermediate step" between a service-connected disability
and a current disability that may be service connected on
a secondary basis under 38 C.F.R. § 3.310(a). VAOGCPREC
1-2017. In such a case, the evidence would need to reflect
that (1) a service-connected disability or disabilities caused
the Veteran to become obese, (2) the obesity was a substantial
factor is causing another disability, and (3) the disability
would not have occurred but for the obesity caused by the
Veteran's service-connected disability or disabilities. Id.

As the Board noted in its first remand in May 2018, the
Veteran also supplemented the record with many medical
articles regarding the relationship between PTSD and sleep
apnea. During his August 2017 Board hearing, the Veteran
noted the studies he submitted that showed that sleep apnea

was secondary to PTSD and asserted that his anxiety and depression caused problems sleeping. In private treatment records dated in February 1999, related to a worker's compensation claim for PTSD, the examiner noted the Veteran's prior motor vehicle accident and reported that the Veteran had sleep apnea, a non-industrial disorder, possibly a side effect from his medication used to treat the PTSD he incurred in 1993 at the time of the accident. The Veteran submitted a copy of a November 2009 traumatic brain injury (TBI) DBQ on which he handwrote that his loss of energy/anergia, changes in sleeping patterns/sleep disturbance, and tiredness/fatigue, noted in the examination report reserved for psychometric testing results and depressive symptoms, were related to, or represented, sleep apnea. He also wrote that the medication used to treat his PTSD helped him sleep.

In a September 2015 Disability Benefits Questionnaire (DBQ), the Veteran's private physician diagnosed the Veteran with OSA and reported that PTSD and major depression were additional diagnoses that pertained to sleep apnea. The physician, however, did not offer an opinion as to whether the Veteran's sleep apnea was proximately caused or aggravated by his service-connected PTSD on a secondary basis. As such, the Board remanded the matter in May 2018 for the Agency of Original Jurisdiction (AOJ) to afford the Veteran an examination to determine the etiology of his OSA. The examiner was asked to opine as to whether it was at least as likely as not that the Veteran's OSA was proximately due to the Veteran's PTSD or aggravated beyond its natural progression by his PTSD, considering any psychotropic medication required to treat such, and side effects thereof, including weight gain.

In a June 2019 DBQ, the examiner noted the Veteran's diagnosis of diabetes mellitus in 2002, and that his initial weight was 273 pounds, though he reduced such to 203 pounds, and that his current body mass index (BMI) was 32. The examiner noted the Veteran's severe motor vehicle accident in 1994, with no other injuries to the head and neck reported, as well as his long history of nasal allergies with oral allergy and prescription nasal spray medication use as well as treatment for yearly sinus infections. The Veteran reported that after he moved to Oregon, in 1997, his wife noticed that his snoring was increased, and he would stop breathing during sleep. The examiner reported that OSA is an anatomic problem of the oropharynx, treated by continuous positive airway pressure (CPAP) to enlarge the airway, and the anatomic obstructive sleep apnea problem is thus not caused or increased by PTSD or stress.

In an April 2020 addendum, the examiner discussed that the Veteran was currently being treated with medications for anxiety and mood. He reported that weight gain and increased obstructive sleep apnea would not usually be associated with any of the medications listed after review of the relevant drug references, and that weight loss would be a more likely side effect. He noted that the Veteran already weighed 273 at the time of his diagnosis of diabetes mellitus and reduced such to 203 with a current BMI of 32, a considerable improvement, however, he continued to need CPAP at his current weight. He concluded that, based on such, it was less likely than not that the Veteran's obstructive sleep apnea is aggravated beyond its natural progression by his PTSD, considering any psychotropic medication required to treat such, and side effects thereof, including weight gain.

The Board determined in its July 2020 remand, however, that the June 2019 and April 2020 opinions were incomplete and remanded the matter again. While the examiner responded to the Veteran's assertion that his psychiatric medications caused weight gain which caused his OSA, he did not address his assertion that he used food to cope with his psychiatric symptoms which caused his weight gain which caused his sleep apnea. Additionally, the examiner did not comment on the many medical articles submitted by the Veteran regarding the relationship between PTSD and sleep apnea; the February 1999 comment of a private examiner that he had sleep apnea, a non-industrial disorder, possibly a side effect from his psychiatric medication used to treat his PTSD; the results of his November 2009 TBI DBQ on which he handwrote that his loss of energy/anergia, changes in sleeping patterns/ sleep disturbance, and tiredness/fatigue, noted in the examination report reserved for psychometric testing results and depressive symptoms, were related to or represented sleep apnea, and that the medication used to treat his PTSD helped him sleep; and the comment of a private examiner in the September 2015 sleep apnea DBQ that PTSD and major depression were additional diagnoses that pertained to sleep apnea.

An additional addendum opinion was provided in February 2021. In April 2021, the Board again found the opinion deficient for several reasons. Firstly, the February 2021 examiner did not comply with the July 2020 remand directive to discuss the Veteran's assertion that he used food to cope with the psychiatric symptoms of PTSD, which caused weight gain and thereby caused his OSA. Furthermore, similar to the April 2020 addendum opinion which the Board found inadequate, the examiner again based his negative opinion on the fact that the Veteran's OSA and its treatment "continued to be present when his weight went down from 273 to 203." However, a "permanent worsening" of a non-service-connected disability is not required to establish secondary service connection on the basis of aggravation (i.e., aggravation may include temporary worsening, or flare-ups, of a disability). See Ward v. Wilkie, 31 Vet. App. 233, 241-42 (2019). Further, as noted by the examiner in the April 2020 opinion, the Veteran's current BMI is 32, which is still considered obese. Therefore, the Board found it irrelevant if the Veteran has lost some weight over the course of the appeal. The issue is whether his obesity is an intermediate step between his PTSD and OSA. Finally, in correspondence received in March 2021 the Veteran asserted that his service-connected diabetes mellitus is a known catalyst for weight gain resulting in OSA.

As such, the matter was remanded for yet another addendum opinion, which was obtained in July 2021. Unfortunately, the examiner's opinion continued to be incomplete. Notably, as to the Veteran's theory that his diabetes resulted in weight gain, thereby causing or aggravating his OSA, the opinion only stated that the Veteran's obesity was an aggravating factor for his diabetes. It did not address his actual argument that diabetes itself is a known catalyst for weight gain. As to the effect of Veteran's PTSD in causing or aggravating OSA, the examiner again only addressed the effects of PTSD medication. Thus, an additional addendum was obtained in December 2021 pursuant to the Board's most recent remand.

After review of this last addendum, and consideration of the fact that a remand for yet an additional opinion may not serve any useful purpose, the Board resolves all doubt in the Veteran's favor in finding that service connection is warranted.

Specifically, while providing the negative opinion that it was less likely than not that the Veteran's obesity cause or aggravated by his PTSD, the examiner did opine in the positive that it was at least as likely as not that the Veteran's diabetes at least aggravated his obesity due to the metabolic effects of insulin sensitivity on a Veteran who already had obesity at the time of his diabetes diagnosis. While the Board acknowledges that the examiner stated that it would be resorting to mere speculation as to whether the Veteran's sleep apnea would still have occurred absent this obesity, she also stated that "it is also possible that he would not have developed OSA without the obesity." The Board reads the examiner's opinion, as a whole, as one sufficient to meet the "at least as likely as not" standard. See 38 U.S.C. § 5107(b); 38 C.F.R. § 3.102. The Board also notes that, while incomplete in that it failed to discuss the relationship between diabetes and weight gain, the previous examiner's opinion in July 2021 clearly opined that it is at least as likely as not that the Veteran's obesity aggravated his OSA.

In sum, while the previous opinions are negative, the Board finds them to be of lesser probative weight in light of their relative incompleteness. In contrast, the Board reads the most recent opinion as one leaning in favor of whether the Veteran's diabetes (but not his PTSD) at least as likely as not aggravated his obesity, and that his OSA would not have occurred if not for this obesity.

Thus, service connection for OSA on a secondary aggravation basis is granted.

Citation Nr: A22004040

By way of history, in a February 2018 legacy rating decision, a Department of Veterans Affairs (VA) Regional Office (RO), in pertinent part, denied service connection for sleep apnea. After receiving additional evidence, the RO confirmed and continued the prior denial in a May 2018 rating decision. 38 C.F.R. § 3.156(b).

Thereafter, in an April 2019 rating decision, issued pursuant to the Appeals Modernization Act (AMA), the agency of original jurisdiction (AOJ) "reopened" the previously denied claim for service connection for sleep apnea and denied it on the merits. The Veteran filed a supplemental claim in June 2019, which was denied in August 2019. He then requested Higher-Level Review (HLR). In September 2019, the AOJ identified a pre-decisional duty to assist error and ordered additional evidentiary development.

Following the requested development, the AOJ entered another decision denying the claim in January 2020. The Veteran timely appealed that decision to the Board of Veterans' Appeals (Board), requesting the hearing review option. See January 2020 VA Form 10182; 38 C.F.R. §§ 20.201, 20.202(b)(2).

In May 2021, the Veteran testified at a virtual Board hearing before the undersigned Veterans Law Judge. A transcript of that hearing has been associated with the record.

Under the AMA, the Veteran had 90 days from the date of the May 2021 hearing to submit additional evidence in support of his appeal. However, in June 2021, he waived the 90-day period. As such, the Board's review is limited to the evidence of record at the time of the January 2020 rating decision, together with his testimony at the May 2021 hearing.

Entitlement to service connection for sleep apnea

The Veteran seeks to establish service connection for sleep apnea. He says that he developed sleep problems while on active duty which either represented, or ultimately matured into, sleep apnea. He has submitted supporting lay statements from his spouse and parents to the effect that he exhibited relevant symptoms contemporaneous with and/or shortly after service. He has also advanced argument to the effect that his sleep apnea is secondary to his service-connected PTSD.

Service connection is warranted where the evidence of record establishes that a particular injury or disease resulting in disability was incurred in the line of duty in the active military service or, if pre-existing such service, was aggravated thereby. 38 U.S.C. § 1110; 38 C.F.R. § 3.303(a).

Generally, in order to prove service connection, there must be competent, credible evidence of (1) a current disability, (2) in-service incurrence or aggravation of an injury or disease, and (3) a nexus, or link, between the current disability and the in-service disease or injury. See, e.g., Davidson v. Shinseki, 581 F.3d 1313 (Fed. Cir. 2009); Pond v. West, 12 Vet. App. 341 (1999).

Under applicable law, disability which is proximately due to or the result of a service-connected disease or injury shall also be service connected. 38 C.F.R. § 3.310(a). Establishing service connection on a secondary basis requires evidence sufficient to show: (1) that a current disability exists; and (2) that the current disability was either (a) caused or (b) aggravated by a service-connected disability. 38 C.F.R. § 3.310; Allen v. Brown, 7 Vet. App. 439 (1995).

The United States Court of Appeals for Veterans Claims (Court) held in Ward v. Wilkie, 31 Vet. App. 233 (2019), that 38 C.F.R. § 3.310(b) (pertaining to aggravation) does not require that there be "permanent worsening" of a nonservice-connected disability. Instead, secondary service connection is warranted for "any incremental increase in disabilityany additional impairment of earning capacityin nonservice-connected disabilities resulting from service-connected conditions, above the degree of disability existing before the increaseregardless of its permanence." Id. at 239.

In adjudicating the Veteran's claim, the Board observes that nothing of record shows that he has the requisite knowledge, skill, experience, training, or education to render medical opinions. Consequently, his contentions cannot constitute competent medical evidence. 38 C.F.R. § 3.159(a)(1).

However, in making all determinations, the Board must fully consider the lay assertions of record. A layperson is competent to report on the onset and recurrence of observable symptoms. See Layno v. Brown, 6 Vet. App. 465, 470 (1994) (a Veteran is competent to report on that of which he or she has personal knowledge). Lay evidence can also be competent and sufficient evidence of a diagnosis or to establish etiology if (1) the layperson is competent to identify the medical condition, (2) the layperson is reporting a contemporaneous medical diagnosis, or (3) lay testimony describing symptoms at the time supports a later diagnosis by a medical professional. Davidson v. Shinseki, 581 F.3d 1313, 1316 (Fed. Cir. 2009). When considering whether lay evidence is competent, the Board must determine, on a case by case basis, whether the Veteran's particular disability is the type of disability for which lay evidence may be competent. Kahana v. Shinseki, 24 Vet. App. 428 (2011).

When there is an approximate balance of positive and negative evidence regarding any issue material to the determination of a matter, the benefit of the doubt shall be given to the claimant. 38 U.S.C. § 5107(b); 38 C.F.R. § 3.102. When a reasonable doubt arises regarding service origin, such doubt will be resolved in the favor of the claimant. An approximate balance of the evidence includes but is not limited to equipoise. Lynch v. McDonough, No. 2020-2067 (Fed. Cir. Dec. 17, 2021). Evidence is not in "approximate balance" or "nearly equal" when the evidence persuasively favors one side or the other. Id.

Initially, the Board observes that the Veteran's service treatment records do not contain any entries reflecting a diagnosis of, or treatment for, sleep apnea. At the May 2021 hearing, he acknowledged that he did not seek in-service treatment for sleep problems, and that sleep apnea was first diagnosed in 2016, several years after his discharge from service. See, e.g., Mense v. Derwinski, 1 Vet. App. 354, 356 (1991) (the absence of any medical records of a diagnosis or treatment for many years after service can be probative evidence against a claim.). Under the circumstances, the Board finds that medical opinion evidence is required to assess the likelihood that the Veteran's sleep apnea developed while on active duty.

Similarly, in regard to the claim for secondary service connection, the effect that PTSD has on sleep apnea involves complex medical questions. Thus, medical opinion evidence is required to resolve that matter as well.

Here, a number of medical opinions are of record. In determining the probative value to be assigned to a medical opinion, the Board must consider three factors. See Nieves-Rodriguez v. Peake, 22 Vet. App. 295 (2008). The initial inquiry in determining probative value is to assess whether a medical expert was fully informed of the pertinent factual premises (i.e., medical history) of the case. A review of the claims file is not required, since a medical professional can also become aware of the relevant medical history by having treated a Veteran for a long period of time or through a factually accurate medical history reported by a Veteran. See Id. at 303-04. The second inquiry involves consideration of whether the medical expert provided a fully articulated opinion. See Id. A medical opinion that is equivocal in nature or expressed in speculative language does not provide the degree of certainty required for medical nexus evidence. See McLendon v. Nicholson, 20 Vet. App. 79 (2006). The third and final factor in determining the probative value of an opinion involves consideration of whether the opinion is supported by a reasoned analysis. The most probative value of a medical opinion comes from its reasoning. Therefore, a medical opinion containing only data and conclusions is not entitled to any weight. In fact, a review of the claims file does not substitute for a lack of a reasoned analysis. See Nieves-Rodriguez, 22 Vet. App. at 304; see also Stefl v. Nicholson, 21 Vet. App. 120, 124 (2007) ("[A] medical opinion . . . must support its conclusion with an analysis that the Board can consider and weigh against contrary opinions.").

Here, medical opinions have been provided by various VA examiners who were familiar with the Veteran's medical history from review of his claims folder. There are also opinions of record from Dr. N., who is familiar with the Veteran's history as his primary VA treating physician. Nothing in the record causes the Board to doubt the qualifications of any of these individuals to provide competent medical opinions, nor has the Veteran contended otherwise.

The evidence in support of the Veteran's appeal includes an April 2018 statement from Dr. N., who opined that the Veteran's sleep apnea was "most likely than not" related to his PTSD. In a December 2018 statement, Dr. N. opined that the sleep apnea was "more likely than not" secondary to PTSD, due to sleep disturbances and nightmares. However, Dr. N. did not provide a substantive rationale in support of either of those opinions.

In a June 2019 statement, Dr. N. again opined the Veteran's sleep apnea was "more likely than not" connected to his PTSD, due to sleep disturbances, nightmares, and respiratory issues due to a history of exposure to burn pits. In support of that opinion, Dr. N. noted that studies had been conducted showing links between PTSD and sleep apnea, with results showing that disruptive sleep/sleep deprivation/ hyperarousal/fragmented sleep and psychological stress play a role in this connection. Dr. N. noted that the Veteran had complained of and experienced these stressors while deployed in Iraq and continued to have the same issues in his present life due to his service-connected PTSD and diagnosis of sleep apnea. Dr. N. further noted that studies showed that Iraq and Afghanistan veterans who were evaluated for PTSD were found to have a 69.2 percent higher risk of sleep apnea.

The Board observes that Dr. N.'s June 2019 statement was

not expressed in speculative or equivocal language, and was supported by stated rational with reference to the record, as well as to pertinent medical treatise evidence.

The evidence against the Veteran's claim includes an April 2019 VA examiner's opinion to the effect that the Veteran's sleep apnea was less likely as not proximately due to or the result of PTSD. The examiner stated there was no medical nexus establishing causality between current complaints and military service; and that no residual or chronic disability subject to service connection was shown by the service treatment records or demonstrated by evidence following service. The examiner also noted that the Veteran was first diagnosed with sleep apnea in 2017, which was after his military service ended in 2010.

An addendum opinion was requested from the April 2019 VA examiner in light of the Veteran's contention of in-service sleep problems, and supporting lay evidence. In June 2019, the VA examiner stated that an opinion could not be provided without resort to speculation.

A subsequent December 2019 medical opinion from a different VA examiner found that the Veteran's sleep apnea was less likely than not (less than 50 percent probability) incurred in or caused by the claimed in-service injury, event, or illness. The examiner's noted, in pertinent part, that there was no sleep study during service to confirm that he had sleep apnea at that time. The examiner also opined that it was less likely than not that the Veteran's sleep apnea was proximately due to or the result of his service-connected PTSD. The examiner acknowledged that PTSD was a risk factor for sleep apnea, but said that it does not cause it. The examiner further noted that although there were common symptoms between the two conditions, they were two separate conditions.

The Board notes that the December 2019 VA examiner's

opinion was not expressed in speculative or equivocal language, and as detailed above, was supported by stated rationale. However, while the examiner provided an opinion against PTSD being the cause of the sleep apnea, the opinion did not explicitly address the matter of secondary aggravation, particularly in light of the holding in Ward, supra. Moreover, it would seem that the the examiner's acknowledgement that PTSD is a "risk factor" for sleep apnea tends to support the possibility of secondary aggravation.

The Board reiterates that the law mandates resolving all reasonable doubt in favor of the claimant. The Court has held that in light of this doctrine, an accurate determination of etiology is not a condition precedent to granting service connection; nor is "definite etiology" or "obvious etiology." Alemany v. Brown, 9 Vet. App. 518 (1996).

Considering the evidence in its totality, the Board is persuaded that there is an approximate balance of evidence regarding whether the Veteran's sleep apnea is secondary to his service-connected PTSD. The appeal is granted.
Citation Nr: 22021527
he Veteran has a current diagnosis of sleep apnea, confirmed as obstructive sleep apnea (OSA) by an in-laboratory polysomnography in June 2011, as well as central sleep apnea. See June 2011 Boston University Diagnostic Report; June 2019 Sleep Apnea Disability Benefits Questionnaire (DBQ). Accordingly, he has a current disability. Davidson, 581 F.3d 1313.

VA medical records reflect that the Veteran has been repeatedly educated on the importance of using his continuous positive airway (CPAP) machine anytime he sleeps. See May 2019 Pulmonary Diagnostic Study Note; December 2019 Neuropsychology Addendum.

The October 2021 Board remand directed the RO to obtain an

adequate medical opinion. The examiner was to specifically consider and address whether the Veteran's sleep-related PTSD symptoms would worsen his sleep apnea symptoms or affect the efficacy of his CPAP therapy in controlling his sleep apnea symptoms.

Following a review of the record, a January 2022 VA medical examiner opined that the Veteran's OSA was less likely than not caused or aggravated by his service-connected PTSD. The examiner rationalized that the Veteran's PTSD symptomatology, including sleep disturbances, would interfere with the use of his CPAP machine. This interference would cause his OSA symptoms to be ameliorated to a lesser extent, but the examiner noted there would be no deleterious effect on the sleep apnea itself. See January 2022 Medical Opinion DBQ.

Although the VA examiner gave a negative nexus opinion, the rationale provided actually supports the opposite conclusion when read carefully. In this regard, the examiner's rationale essentially states that the sleep disturbances caused by the Veteran's PTSD reduces the effectiveness of his CPAP therapy. A less effective session of CPAP therapy would then reduce the usual improvement of the Veteran's OSA symptoms. Although the examiner stated this reduction would not have any harmful effect on the sleep apnea itself, they did not provide an explanation for this finding.

Accordingly, the Board finds that the Veteran's PTSD aggravates his OSA. In this regard, there is evidence showing that the Veteran's sleep related PTSD symptoms reduce the efficacy of his CPAP therapy which aggravates his OSA symptoms.

The Board acknowledges that there are negative opinions of record in the form of VA opinions dated June 2019, April 2021, and August 2021. As these examinations did not fully address the impact of the Veteran's PTSD on his sleep apnea, the Board finds these opinions inadequate. See Wilson v. Derwinski, 2 Vet. App. 614 (1992).

In sum, the Board finds that the evidence for an against the claim that the Veteran's OSA is aggravated by his service-connected PTSD is evenly balanced. When the evidence for and against a claim is in relative equipoise, by law, the Board must resolve all reasonable doubt in favor of the Veteran. See 38 U.S.C. § 1154(b); 5107; 38 C.F.R. § 3.102; see also Gilbert v. Derwinski, 1 Vet. App. 49, 55 (1990). Therefore, the benefit of the doubt must be resolved in favor of the Veteran and entitlement to service connection for obstructive sleep apnea, as secondary to service-connected PTSD, is warranted.

Citation Nr: 22005918

Generally, service connection may be granted for a disability resulting from a disease or injury incurred in or aggravated by active service. 38 U.S.C. §§ 1110, 1131; 38 C.F.R. § 3.303. The three-element test for service connection requires evidence of: (1) a current disability; (2) in-service incurrence or aggravation of a disease or injury; and (3) a causal relationship between the current disability and the in-service disease or injury. Shedden v. Principi, 381 F.3d 1163, 1166 -67 (Fed. Cir. 2004).

A disability which is proximately due to or the result of a service-connected disease shall be service connected. 38 C.F.R. § 3.310(a). A claimant is also entitled to service connection on a secondary basis when it is shown that a service-connected disability has aggravated a nonservice-connected disability. Allen v. Brown, 7 Vet. App. 439 (1995).

While obesity is not a disability per se, obesity may be an "intermediate step" between a service-connected disability and a current disability that may be connected on a secondary basis. In order to meet this criteria, the veteran must demonstrate affirmative answers to the following inquiry: (1) that a previously service-connected disability caused him to become obese; (2) that obesity was a substantial factor in causing secondary disability; and (3) the secondary disability would only have occurred but for the obesity. VAOPGCPREC 1-2017 (January 6, 2017); See Walsh v. Wilkie, 32 Vet. App. 300 (2020).

In Garner v. Tran, the Court of Appeals for Veterans Claims (Court) set forth a non-exhaustive list of considerations that could give rise to a reasonably raised theory of secondary service connection with obesity as an intermediate step: (1) mobility limitations or reduced physical activity as a result of a service-connected physical disability; (2) reduced physical activity or inability to follow a course of exercise or diet as a result of service-connected mental disability; (3) side effects of medication where the medication is prescribed for a service-connected disability; (4) treatise evidence suggesting a connection between all or some combination of obesity, service-connected disability, and the claimed condition; (5) lay statements by a veteran attributing weight gain or obesity to the service-connected disability; and (6) statements by treating physicians or medical examiners attributing weight gain or obesity to the service-connected disability. The Court explained the critical commonality among the nonprecedential decisions was that "there is some evidence in the record which draws an association or suggests a relationship between the veteran's obesity, or weight gain resulting in obesity, and a service-connected condition."

In determining whether service connection is warranted for a disability, VA is responsible for determining whether the evidence supports the claim or is in relative equipoise, with the Veteran prevailing in either event, or whether a preponderance of the evidence is against the claim, in which case the claim is denied. 38 U.S.C. § 5107; 38 C.F.R. § 3.102; Gilbert v. Derwinski, 1 Vet. App. 49 (1990).

Entitlement to service connection for obstructive sleep apnea as secondary to PTSD is granted.

The Veteran specifically contends that her obstructive sleep apnea symptoms were undiagnosed while in service. In the alternative, she contends that her obstructive sleep apnea is proximately due to or aggravated by her service-connected disabilities, and/or proximately due to or the result of obesity that is proximately due to her service-connected disabilities. See September 2020 Appellate Brief. In the July 2020 Statement in Support of Claim, the Veteran's friend noted that she would fall asleep in noisy environments or while speaking in a conversation, as well as, would snore loudly while she sleeps to emphasize that the Veteran had a sleep problem during service.

A January 1997 service treatment record reflects the Veteran's complaints of fatigue that was noted to be possibly related to her past history of anemia, as it was noted that the Veteran was previously diagnosed with anemia. A March 1997 service treatment record noted that the Veteran had complained of a "tired feeling" that she had been experiencing "on and off" for two months. She was diagnosed with fatigue. In April 1999, she was assessed for anemia.

Post-service treatment records indicate that the Veteran was diagnosed with obstructive sleep apnea in May 2013 during a sleep study. It was also noted that she had symptoms of daytime fatigue, obesity and depression. The provider also noted that there was a question of whether the Veteran had narcolepsy while in service as she was falling asleep easily, but she was not formally diagnosed.

A July 2021 VA examiner opined that the Veteran's obstructive sleep apnea was less likely as not aggravated beyond its natural progression by PTSD. The examiner noted that the Veteran had a body mass index (BMI) of 35 at the time of the sleep study. The examiner emphasized that obesity is the greatest risk factor in developing sleep apnea and that there is no literature that suggests that PTSD or any psychiatric condition aggravates obstructive sleep apnea in the setting of high BMI. The examiner reasoned that in the study titled "Post-traumatic stress disorder predicts future weight change in the Millennium Cohort Study," it is noted that PTSD is independently associated with a higher risk of weight gain and loss, the former of which leads to a higher prevalence of overweight and obesity and a higher risk of comorbidities associated with excessive body adiposity. The examiner noted that the Veteran's PTSD likely contributed to the elevated BMI but did not have a direct effect on the obstructive sleep apnea. Therefore, the examiner found that the claimed obstructive sleep apnea was not aggravated beyond its natural progression by PTSD.

Further, the July 2021 VA examiner opined that there is no other condition that is currently service-connected that would be a direct cause or aggravation of obstructive sleep apnea. The examiner noted that in the same study titled "Post-traumatic stress disorder predicts future weight change in the Millennium Cohort Study," PTSD was found to be independently associated with a higher risk of weight gain and loss, the former of which leads to a higher prevalence of overweight and obesity and a higher risk of comorbidities associated with excessive body adiposity. The examiner concludes that the PTSD likely contributed to weight gain which led to obstructive sleep apnea. The Board finds that July 2021 VA examiner considered all evidence of record after thorough review of the claims file, including lay statements properly weighed. See Nieves-Rodriguez v. Peake, 22 Vet. App. 295 (2009); Stefl v. Nicholson, 21 Vet. App. 120, 124

(2007) ("[A] medical opinion...must support its conclusion with an analysis the Board can consider and weight against contrary opinion"). Furthermore, the medical examination report contained clear conclusions with supporting data and a thorough rationale. See Nieves-Rodriguez v. Peake, supra. Therefore, the medical opinion is of great probative value.

Although the July 2021 examiner did not conclude that the Veteran's obstructive sleep apnea was caused or aggravated by her service connected PTSD, the Board notes that the examiner emphasized that the Veteran's PTSD likely contributed to weight gain which led to the Veteran's obstructive sleep apnea. The Board also notes that the May 2020 examiner emphasized the same understanding that medical literature shows that there is an increased risk of those with PTSD to have obstructive sleep apnea. Obesity may be an "intermediate step" in a secondary service-connection analysis when the service-connected disability causes or aggravates obesity under 38 C.F.R. § 3.310(a). See also Garner v. Tran, supra.

Here, the July 2021 VA examiner cited medical articles or treatise that drew connection between PTSD and obesity, whereas obesity became an intermediate step to the Veteran's obstructive sleep apnea. Thus, in reaching the foregoing determinations, the Board has applied the benefit of the doubt doctrine and resolved all doubt in the Veteran's favor. The Board finds that entitlement to service connection for obstructive sleep apnea is warranted. 38 U.S.C. § 5107; 38 C.F.R. § 3.102; Gilbert v. Derwinski, supra. Service connection for obstructive sleep apnea is granted.

Citation Nr: 22005456

By way of background, the Veteran reported in an April 2012 statement that he used food to cope with his stress and anxiety, which led to problems with sleep apnea. In his December 2013 Notice of Disagreement, the Veteran asserted that the psychotropic medications he was prescribed for his PTSD caused weight gain which caused sleep apnea. The Board notes that, while obesity cannot be service-connected on a direct basis, and obesity cannot qualify as an in-service event for service connection purposes, obesity may indeed serve as an "intermediate step" between a service-connected disability and a current disability that may be service connected on a secondary basis under 38 C.F.R. § 3.310(a). VAOGCPREC 1-2017. In such a case, the evidence would need to reflect that (1) a service-connected disability or disabilities caused the Veteran to become obese, (2) the obesity was a substantial factor is causing another disability, and (3) the disability would not have occurred but for the obesity caused by the Veteran's service-connected disability or disabilities. Id.

As the Board noted in its first remand in May 2018, the Veteran also supplemented the record with many medical articles regarding the relationship between PTSD and sleep apnea. During his August 2017 Board hearing, the Veteran noted the studies he submitted that showed that sleep apnea was secondary to PTSD and asserted that his anxiety and depression caused problems sleeping. In private treatment records dated in February 1999, related to a worker's compensation claim for PTSD, the examiner noted the Veteran's prior motor vehicle accident and reported that the Veteran had sleep apnea, a non-industrial disorder, possibly a side effect from his medication used to treat the PTSD he incurred in 1993 at the time of the accident. The Veteran submitted a copy of a November 2009 traumatic brain injury (TBI) DBQ on which he handwrote that his loss of energy/ anergia, changes in sleeping patterns/sleep disturbance, and tiredness/fatigue, noted in the examination report reserved for psychometric testing results and depressive symptoms, were related to, or represented, sleep apnea. He also wrote that the medication used to treat his PTSD helped him sleep.

In a September 2015 Disability Benefits Questionnaire (DBQ), the Veteran's private physician diagnosed the Veteran with OSA and reported that PTSD and major depression were additional diagnoses that pertained to sleep apnea. The physician, however, did not offer an opinion as to whether the Veteran's sleep apnea was proximately caused or aggravated by his service-connected PTSD on a secondary basis. As such, the Board remanded the matter in May 2018 for the Agency of Original Jurisdiction (AOJ) to afford the Veteran an examination to determine the etiology of his OSA. The examiner was asked to opine as to whether it was at least as likely as not that the Veteran's OSA was proximately due to the Veteran's PTSD or aggravated beyond its natural progression by his PTSD, considering any psychotropic medication required to treat such, and side effects thereof, including weight gain.

In a June 2019 DBQ, the examiner noted the Veteran's diagnosis of diabetes mellitus in 2002, and that his initial weight was 273 pounds, though he reduced such to 203 pounds, and that his current body mass index (BMI) was 32. The examiner noted the Veteran's severe motor vehicle accident in 1994, with no other injuries to the head and neck reported, as well as his long history of nasal allergies with oral allergy and prescription nasal spray medication use as well as treatment for yearly sinus infections. The Veteran reported that after he moved to Oregon, in 1997, his wife noticed that his snoring was increased, and he would stop breathing during sleep. The examiner reported that OSA is an anatomic problem of the oropharynx, treated by continuous positive airway pressure (CPAP) to enlarge the airway, and the anatomic obstructive sleep apnea problem is thus not caused or increased by PTSD or stress.

In an April 2020 addendum, the examiner discussed that

the Veteran was currently being treated with medications for anxiety and mood. He reported that weight gain and increased obstructive sleep apnea would not usually be associated with any of the medications listed after review of the relevant drug references, and that weight loss would be a more likely side effect. He noted that the Veteran already weighed 273 at the time of his diagnosis of diabetes mellitus and reduced such to 203 with a current BMI of 32, a considerable improvement, however, he continued to need CPAP at his current weight. He concluded that, based on such, it was less likely than not that the Veteran's obstructive sleep apnea is aggravated beyond its natural progression by his PTSD, considering any psychotropic medication required to treat such, and side effects thereof, including weight gain.

The Board determined in its July 2020 remand, however, that the June 2019 and April 2020 opinions were incomplete and remanded the matter again. While the examiner responded to the Veteran's assertion that his psychiatric medications caused weight gain which caused his OSA, he did not address his assertion that he used food to cope with his psychiatric symptoms which caused his weight gain which caused his sleep apnea. Additionally, the examiner did not comment on the many medical articles submitted by the Veteran regarding the relationship between PTSD and sleep apnea; the February 1999 comment of a private examiner that he had sleep apnea, a non-industrial disorder, possibly a side effect from his psychiatric medication used to treat his PTSD; the results of his November 2009 TBI DBQ on which he handwrote that his loss of energy/anergia, changes in sleeping patterns/ sleep disturbance, and tiredness/fatigue, noted in the examination report reserved for psychometric testing results and depressive symptoms, were related to or represented sleep apnea, and that the medication used to treat his PTSD helped him sleep; and the comment of a private examiner in the September 2015 sleep apnea DBQ that PTSD and major depression were additional diagnoses that pertained to sleep apnea.

An additional addendum opinion was provided in February 2021. In April 2021, the Board again found the opinion deficient for several reasons. Firstly, the February 2021 examiner did not comply with the July 2020 remand directive to discuss the Veteran's assertion that he used food to cope with the psychiatric symptoms of PTSD, which caused weight gain and thereby caused his OSA. Furthermore, similar to the April 2020 addendum opinion which the Board found inadequate, the examiner again based his negative opinion on the fact that the Veteran's OSA and its treatment "continued to be present when his weight went down from 273 to 203." However, a "permanent worsening" of a non-service-connected disability is not required to establish secondary service connection on the basis of aggravation (i.e., aggravation may include temporary worsening, or flare-ups, of a disability). See Ward v. Wilkie, 31 Vet. App. 233, 241-42 (2019). Further, as noted by the examiner in the April 2020 opinion, the Veteran's current BMI is 32, which is still considered obese. Therefore, the Board found it irrelevant if the Veteran has lost some weight over the course of the appeal. The issue is whether his obesity is an intermediate step between his PTSD and OSA. Finally, in correspondence received in March 2021 the Veteran asserted that his service-connected diabetes mellitus is a known catalyst for weight gain resulting in OSA.

As such, the matter was remanded for yet another addendum opinion, which was obtained in July 2021. Unfortunately, the examiner's opinion continued to be incomplete. Notably, as to the Veteran's theory that his diabetes resulted in weight gain, thereby causing or aggravating his OSA, the opinion only stated that the Veteran's obesity was an aggravating factor for his diabetes. It did not address his actual argument that diabetes itself is a known catalyst for weight gain. As to the effect of Veteran's PTSD in causing or aggravating OSA, the examiner again only addressed the effects of PTSD medication. Thus, an additional addendum was obtained in December 2021 pursuant to the Board's most recent remand.

After review of this last addendum, and consideration of the fact that a remand for yet an additional opinion may not serve any useful purpose, the Board resolves all doubt in the Veteran's favor in finding that service connection is warranted.

Specifically, while providing the negative opinion that it was less likely than not that the Veteran's obesity cause or aggravated by his PTSD, the examiner did opine in the positive that it was at least as likely as not that the Veteran's diabetes at least aggravated his obesity due to the metabolic effects of insulin sensitivity on a Veteran who already had obesity at the time of his diabetes diagnosis. While the Board acknowledges that the examiner stated that it would be resorting to mere speculation as to whether the Veteran's sleep apnea would still have occurred absent this obesity, she also stated that "it is also possible that he would not have developed OSA without the obesity." The Board reads the examiner's opinion, as a whole, as one sufficient to meet the "at least as likely as not" standard. See 38 U.S.C. § 5107(b); 38 C.F.R. § 3.102. The Board also notes that, while incomplete in that it failed to discuss the relationship between diabetes and weight gain, the previous examiner's opinion in July 2021 clearly opined that it is at least as likely as not that the Veteran's obesity aggravated his OSA.

In sum, while the previous opinions are negative, the Board finds them to be of lesser probative weight in light of their relative incompleteness. In contrast, the Board reads the most recent opinion as one leaning in favor of whether the Veteran's diabetes (but not his PTSD) at least as likely as not aggravated his obesity, and that his OSA would not have occurred if not for this obesity.

Thus, service connection for OSA on a secondary aggravation basis is granted.

Citation Nr: 22002916

In September 2014, the Veteran was administered a Sleep Apnea Disability Benefits Questionnaire (Sleep Apnea DBQ). Following the examination, the examiner opined that the Veteran's obstructive sleep apnea is likely due to his physical attributes, thick neck, and small oropharynx and less likely than not related to his service, to include any exposure during his service in Southwest Asia. In favor of the opinion, the examiner reasoned that "physiologically, there is no evidence to support a specific exposure event relating to the development of obstructive sleep apnea." See Sleep Apnea DBQ of September 2014. The Board finds the examiner's opinion that the Veteran's sleep apnea is related to his "physical attributes" adequate and assigns it high probative value, in view of the other evidence of record.

In September 2015, the Veteran submitted a medical opinion that noted a strong correlation between sleep apnea and PTSD and summarized pertinent medical literature. The opinion was accompanied by various articles detailing research findings regarding a possible correlation between sleep apnea and PTSD. See medical opinion of September 2015 and associated literature. It is observed that while this medical opinion indicated that there was a strong correlation between sleep apnea and PTSD, the subscriber did not clearly opine whether the Veteran's sleep apnea was at least as likely as not related to the Veteran's PTSD.

In June 2017, the Veteran submitted another medical opinion that noted the Veteran's service-connected back and fibromyalgia disabilities cause pain with mobility, which in turn diminish the Veteran's ability to exercise and maintain a healthy weight. The subscriber noted that the Veteran's physical limitations due to his service-connected disabilities coupled with his physical attributes of an enlarged neck and crowded oropharynx due to his weight, contribute to his sleep apnea. Furthermore, the subscriber noted that the Veteran's PTSD causes sleep continuity instability which contributes to the Veteran's sleep apnea condition. Thus, the subscriber opined that it is at least as likely as not that the Veteran's service-connected disabilities caused his sleep apnea. See medical opinion of June 2017. The Board interprets the subscriber's opinion as one in favor of the claim, associating the Veteran's sleep apnea to his weight and associating his weight gain to his service-connected disabilities which limit the Veteran's mobility and physical activity. The Board finds this medical opinion adequate and assigns it high probative value, in light of the other evidence of record. The Board observes the June 2017 medical opinion does not specifically address the physical limitations the Veteran suffers due to his service-connected disabilities or the extent of such limitations, beyond what was noted above. However, the record contains various examination reports pertaining to the Veteran's service-connected back disability and his fibromyalgia, which do show the Veteran experiences physical limitations due to his service-connected disabilities. For example, a Fibromyalgia DBQ, notes the Veteran experiences decreased exercise tolerance and increased pain with exercise due to his fibromyalgia disability. See Fibromyalgia DBQ, completed by a private provider, associated with the claims file in May 2016. Similarly, the Veteran's most recent Back DBQ shows reports of daily flares that limit his mobility. See Back DBQ associated with the claims file in November 2021.

Based on the above and the other evidence of record, the Board finds that the evidence is at least in equipoise as to whether service connection for sleep apnea on a secondary basis is warranted.

First, the Board observes that the Veteran has a diagnosis of sleep apnea. See generally VA medical records. Further, the Veteran is currently service connected for a back disability, fibromyalgia and for PTSD, among other disabilities. As such, his claim meets the first and second requirements for service connection on a secondary basis, a current disability (sleep apnea) and service-connected disabilities (back disability, fibromyalgia, and PTSD).

Thus, the remaining question before the Board is whether the probative evidence of record provides a medical nexus between the sleep apnea and the service-connected disabilities. Here, the Board finds that the evidence of record is at least in equipoise as to whether the Veteran's sleep apnea is caused by his service-connected disabilities which cause physical impairments and have caused weight-gain, and as to whether the Veteran's PTSD contributes to the sleep apnea disability.

Notably, the VA examiner that subscribed the medical opinion of September 2014 noted that the Veteran's sleep apnea is likely due to his physical attributes of thick neck and small oropharynx. See Sleep apnea DBQ of September 2014.

Additionally, the June 2017 medical opinion noted how the Veteran's service-connected back and fibromyalgia disabilities limit his ability to exercise and maintain a healthy weight. Further, this medical opinion noted how the Veteran's weight causes or contributes to his enlarged neck and crowded oropharynx, in addition to noting that his PTSD causes sleep impairment which in turn aggravates or contributes to his sleep apnea. See medical opinion of June 2017. There is no other probative medical opinion of record that addresses the Veteran's sleep apnea and its possible connection to his weight and/or other service-connected disabilities.

Accordingly, the Board finds that the probative evidence of record is at least in equipoise as to whether the Veteran's PTSD contributes to his sleep apnea, as well as to whether his weight gain is caused by his service-connected back and fibromyalgia disabilities and associated physical limitations. Further, the evidence is at least in equipoise as to whether the Veteran's weight is a substantial factor that causes sleep apnea since his weight has been found to be a contributing factor to his thick neck and small (or crowded) oropharynx which are "physical attributes" that have been found to cause his sleep apnea. Finally, the evidence is at least in equipoise as to whether the Veteran's sleep apnea would not have occurred but for the obesity caused by his service-connected disabilities.

Thus, resolving reasonable doubt in the Veteran's favor, the Board finds that service connection for sleep apnea on a secondary basis is warranted as the evidence of record is at least in equipoise as to whether his sleep apnea is at least as likely as not caused by service-connected back, fibromyalgia disabilities that have caused physical limitations and weight gain, as well as his PTSD symptomatology.

Citation Nr: A22003123

The Veteran asserts that his sleep apnea is secondary to his service-connected PTSD.

Private treatment records reflect that the Veteran was diagnosed with sleep apnea after a July 2014 sleep study. In a September 2021 private opinion, a private examiner opined that the Veteran's PTSD likely had a profound impact on the development and subsequent substantial aggravation of the Veteran's sleep apnea. Review of the August 2018 rating decision and March 2019 Higher-Level Review rating decision in this case does not reflect that a VA examination specifically for sleep apnea was ordered or conducted. The record shows that the Veteran was afforded a VA Respiratory Conditions examination in July 2018, but that examination primarily addressed the Veteran's asthma, for which service connection is already in effect. Thus, there is no VA opinion to negate the September 2021 private opinion, which the Board finds probative as it addresses the Veteran's medical history and currently diagnosed sleep apnea.

Upon review of the record, the Board finds the evidence establishes that the Veteran's current sleep apnea is aggravated by his service-connected PTSD. Accordingly, after resolving all doubt in favor of the Veteran, the Board finds that service connection for sleep apnea is warranted. 38 U.S.C. § 5107; 38 C.F.R. § 3.102."

Citation Nr: 22005209

In December 2021, the Veteran submitted a private medical opinion from D.B., M.D., who is board-certified in otolaryngology and sleep medicine and specializes in the evaluation and management of obstructive sleep apnea. Dr. B. opined that the Veteran's sleep apnea is at least as likely as not caused by his service-connected PTSD. In support of his opinion, Dr. B. cited to studies demonstrating that veterans with PTSD have a higher prevalence of obstructive sleep apnea than the general population and that the probability of developing obstructive sleep apnea increases with the severity of PTSD symptoms. He indicated that the extreme stress associated with PTSD begins a series of neurochemical changes that cause sleep fragmentation and recurrent arousals, which causes upper airway instability and contributes to the development or worsening of obstructive sleep apnea. Dr. B. additionally stated that the Veteran's PTSD symptoms result in reduced continuous positive airway pressure (CPAP) machine adherence. He cited to a study showing that soldiers with obstructive sleep apnea and comorbid PTSD had significantly decreased CPAP use due to nightmares, mask discomfort, air hunger, and claustrophobia.

He also indicated that the Veteran reported that he often takes off his CPAP because he feels claustrophobic. For these reasons, Dr. B. opined that it is at least as likely as not that the Veteran's obstructive sleep apnea was caused by his service-connected PTSD.

After considering the relevant evidence, the Board finds that the record weighs in favor of finding that the Veteran's obstructive sleep apnea was caused by his service-connected PTSD. In this regard, the Veteran has submitted a credible medical opinion from a competent physician supporting a causal connection between his PTSD and sleep apnea. Dr. B. specifically indicated that PTSD causes neurochemical changes that result in sleep fragmentation and recurrent arousals, which in turn lead to upper airway instability and the development of obstructive sleep apnea. He supported his conclusions with several medical studies and references to the Veteran's medical treatment records. The Board finds that his medical opinion is adequate and assigns great evidentiary weight to his opinion, especially in light of his qualifications and expertise in obstructive sleep apnea. See Nieves-Rodriguez, 22 Vet. App. at 304; Owens, 7 Vet. App. at 433.

The Board finds that the April 2019 VA medical opinion is inadequate because the examiner failed to address the Veteran's and his wife's statements regarding the continuity of his sleep apnea symptoms since his return from Southwest Asia. See Nieves-Rodriguez, 22 Vet. App. at 304. Regardless of the April 2019 medical opinion's inadequacy, no VA opinion has been issued regarding secondary service connection. Given the absence of evidence contradicting Dr. B.'s positive nexus opinion, the Board finds that service connection for obstructive sleep apnea is warranted on a causation basis.

Citation Nr: 22003130

The Veteran contends that his sleep apnea is secondary to PTSD. VA medical treatment records show diagnoses of sleep apnea and a sleep study has confirmed the Veteran's diagnosis. The Veteran is service connected for PTSD.

The remaining question is whether the Veteran's sleep apnea is proximately due to or aggravated by the Veteran's service-connected PTSD.

In December 2015, the Veteran was provided a VA examination for sleep apnea. The prior Board decision found the VA examination inadequate because the report did not include a diagnosis of sleep apnea and a subsequent study confirmed sleep apnea.

In January 2020, another VA medical opinion was provided; the examiner provided a negative etiological opinion, finding that the medical literature did not support that PTSD caused or worsened sleep apnea. The examiner did not discuss the Veteran's PTSD medications, rendering the opinion inadequate.

Further, contrary to the examiner's assertions, the Board is aware of peer-reviewed studies that show the potential neurochemical effects of PTSD on sleep apnea, and indicate a likelihood that PTSD can cause or aggravate sleep apnea by altering the chemical controllers of the musculature of the throat. See, e.g., Leszek Kubin, Neural Control of the Upper Airway: Respiratory and State-Dependent Mechanisms. Compr. Physiol. vol. 6, 4, 1801-1850 (15 Sep. 2016); Rajesh Kumar, Neural Alterations Associated with Anxiety Symptoms in Obstructive Sleep Apnea Syndrome. Depress. Anxiety vol. 26, 5, 480-91 (2009). Both studies are readily available through the National Library of Medicine (https://www.nlm.nih.gov/).

Given that awareness, the relevancy of the studies, the

governmental aspect of availability, and the reasonableness of locating such, the Board finds the studies to be constructively of record. See Euzebio, 989 F.3d 1305, 1321-22 (Fed. Cir. 2021). As the VA medical opinion is not adequate and has no probative value, the medical evidence of record, actual and constructive, must be found to support the claim

Review of the evidence of record also shows that the Veteran is service connected for lung cancer, currently rated 100 percent disabling. VA medical treatment records include pulmonary studies, demonstrating reduced pulmonary functioning. A May 2020 VA examination report also includes pulmonary function test results demonstrating the reduced pulmonary function. The Board recognizes that as an adjudicator, it may not make a medical determination. See Colvin v. Derwinski, 1 Vet. App. 171 (1991) (holding that the rating board cannot substitute its own medical judgment for that of medical professionals). However, the Board may review the evidence of record, evaluate its probative value and draw conclusions from the review. It is reasonable to conclude, without specialized medical expertise or knowledge, that diminished pulmonary function from service-connected lung cancer would worsen the Veteran's symptoms of sleep apnea.

Though the Board could remand this case again for a new opinion, when taking into account the unique circumstances of this particular veteran's medical picture, and considering both the Veteran's PTSD and lung cancer, the Board finds that it is reasonable to conclude that the evidence is in relative equipoise as to whether the Veteran's service-connected disabilities caused the Veteran's sleep apnea. The Board will resolve the benefit of the doubt in favor of the Veteran and finds that service connection is warranted for sleep apnea.

Citation Nr: A22001074

The Veteran seeks service connection of sleep apnea, which

he asserts has been caused or aggravated by his service-connected PTSD. Affording the complete benefit of the doubt, the Board finds that the claim should be granted.

Initially, the Board recognizes a present diagnosis of sleep apnea, as well as service-connection of PTSD.

In support of his appeal, the Veteran has submitted significant evidence, to include multiple scholarly articles discussing the connection between the two disabilities, previous BVA decisions addressing similar questions (the Board again notes that its prior decisions are not precedential and do not bind the Board to a similar outcome in any specific case), a physical examination report, and a medical opinion by the examining private physician. The private physician opined that the claimed sleep apnea was at least as likely as not due to or the result of the Veteran's service -connected PTSD. In support of this conclusion, the examiner noted the wide history of research on PTSD and its effects on a person's sleep, specifically that PTSD can aggravate sleep apnea symptoms and leads to additional sleep apnea in veterans. The examiner also cited to two scholarly articles which find in support of his opinion.

VA subsequently sought its own opinion regarding the Veterans claim. In May 2020, a VA examiner reviewed the available medical evidence and concluded that the claimed sleep apnea was less likely than not caused by or the result of the Veteran's service-connected condition. In support of this the examiner noted that the Veteran's service treatment records were negative for any sleep apnea symptoms. He also noted that medical articles show that PTSD and sleep apnea may co-exist and that sleep apnea is more prevalent in individuals with depression, however, studies do not demonstrate direct causality or mechanism on how PTSD or depression can actually cause sleep apnea. It is further noted that the VA examiner dismissed the private examiner's opinion noting that he discussed aggravation but not direct causation. The VA examiner did not discuss possible aggravation of sleep apnea by the service-connected PTSD.

Ultimately, affording the complete benefit of the doubt, the Board will find that the private opinion is slightly more persuasive than the VA opinion. In this regard, while not explicitly stating so, the private examiner did discuss aggravation of the Veteran's sleep apnea, clearly implying that the sleep apnea was more likely than not aggravated by his PTSD. To the extent that the VA examiner noted this conclusion, he failed to refute it or discuss this possible theory of service connection, instead focusing explicitly on direct causation. In this regard, the Board notes that secondary service connection may be established on either direct causation or aggravation basis. To the extent that the private opinion does consider aggravation, while the VA opinion does not, the Board finds the private opinion more persuasive of the question at hand. At the very least, the medical evidence is in relative equipoise as to whether the sleep apnea disorder has been caused and/or aggravated by his service-connected PTSD. When the evidence is in equipoise, the claimant should prevail. As such, the Board finds that the claim should be granted.

The Board's decision in this case is binding only with respect to the instant matter decided. This decision is not precedential and does not establish VA policies or interpretations of general applicability. 38 C.F.R. § 20.1303.

Citation Nr: A22001066

The Veteran asserts that service connection is warranted for obstructive sleep apnea on the theory that the disability was caused or aggravated by his service-connected PTSD. His service treatment records show no reports or diagnoses of sleep apnea.

An October 2019 private examination report conducted by a physician noted that the Veteran's claim files as well as medical literature were reviewed. The physician reported that after extensive medical research, review of claims file, and clinical experience, that it was at least as likely as not that the Veteran PTSD caused sleeping disfunction and sleep apnea. The physician cited to numerous medical studies and literature to support the rationale and opinion provided that the Veteran's sleep apnea was caused by service-connected PTSD.

In March 2021, a VA examiner opined that, after a review of the evidence of record, it was less likely than not that sleep apnea was caused by the Veteran's service-connected PTSD. The VA examiner remarked that the conditions of sleep apnea and PTSD were not medically related. The VA examiner reported that sleep apnea was a separate entity from the PTSD and a thorough review of medical literature failed to demonstrate a causal relationship.

In reviewing the evidence of record, the Board finds that the evidence is at least in equipoise regarding the Veteran's claim of entitlement to service connection for sleep apnea, as secondary to the service-connected PTSD. When there is an approximate balance of positive and negative evidence regarding any issue material to the determination of a matter, reasonable doubt shall be resolved in favor of the claimant. 38 U.S.C. § 5107(b). When a reasonable doubt arises regarding service origin, that doubt will be resolved in the favor of the claimant. Reasonable doubt is doubt which exists because of an approximate balance of positive and negative evidence which does not satisfactorily prove or disprove the claim. An accurate determination of etiology is not a condition precedent to granting service connection, nor is definite etiology or obvious etiology. Alemany v. Brown, 9 Vet. App. 518 (1996); 38 U.S.C. § 5107(b). Further, a veteran need only demonstrate that there is an approximate balance of positive and negative evidence to prevail. Entitlement need not be established beyond a reasonable doubt, by clear and convincing evidence, or by a fair preponderance of the evidence. When the evidence is in relative equipoise, the law dictates that the appellant prevails.

The Board is aware of the conflicting medical evidence as to whether the Veteran's current sleep apnea was caused by his service-connected PTSD. However, the Board concludes that in this case, as it now stands, the evidence of record is at least in relative equipoise. The Board finds that none of the medical opinions are more probative than the other opinions of record. The Veteran's October 2019 private evaluation shows that the sleep apnea was caused by service-connected PTSD. The March 2021 VA examiner, in contrast, determined that the Veteran's sleep apnea was not caused by PTSD. Each medical opinion is supported by a reasoned analysis of medical facts. Neives-Rodriguuez v. Peake, 22 Vet. App. 295 (2008).

The Board finds that the medical opinions and diagnoses in this case are at least in equipoise as to whether the Veteran's sleep apnea was caused by his service-connected PTSD. When evidence is in relative equipoise, reasonable doubt must be decided in the appellant's favor. Accordingly, resolving all reasonable doubt in favor of the Veteran, the Board finds that service connection for a sleep apnea secondary to PTSD is warranted.

Citation Nr: A22000192

The Board finds that the evidence is at least in equipoise that the Veteran's obstructive sleep apnea is proximately due to his service-connected acquired psychiatric disability.

In May 2019, the Veteran's private doctor submitted a medical opinion for sleep apnea on the Veteran's behalf. The physician indicated that the Veteran's obstructive sleep apnea is, potentially, directly correlated with the progression of PTSD. The examiner cited a study that the probability of having a higher risk of OSA increased with the severity of PTSD symptoms. The examiner also explained that the medical literature supports a direct correlation between the onset and progression of PTSD.

In September 2019, the Veteran was afforded a VA examination for sleep apnea. The examiner indicated that the Veteran was diagnosed with obstructive sleep apnea and the Veteran requires the use of a CPAP. The Veteran symptoms included persistent daytime hypersomnolence. The examiner opined that the Veteran's obstructive sleep apnea is less likely than not (less than 50% probability) proximately due to or the result of the Veteran's service-connected PTSD. The examiner cited several studies and indicated that the literature is inconclusive. For example, the examiner cited, "no conclusions can be drawn from the data currently available on the potential relationship between [sleep disordered breathing] and PTSD...an association, though inconsistent, between PTSD and SDB without clarity as to whether sleep apnea predisposes to PTSD or the other way around... More recently, another report reviewed prior studies showing high co-morbidity between OSA and PTSD and found all had a moderate to high risk of selection bias, which would overestimate the relationship." The examiner concluded that due to the lack of scientific evidence supporting the causal role for PTSD in the development of sleep apnea, obstructive sleep apnea was less likely than not caused by the Veteran's currently service-connected PTSD. The examiner also indicated that the Veteran was obese, and that the Veteran exaggerated his symptoms. The examiner opined that the development of obstructive sleep apnea was less likely than not aggravated beyond its natural course by the Veteran's service-connected PTSD. As to the rationale, the examiner cited the previously cited research studies and concluded that there is a lack of scientific evidence supporting aggravation beyond its natural course by the Veteran's service-connected PTSD. The examiner discussed the conflicting evidence submitted by the Veteran's private physician. The September 2019 VA examiner indicated that the private physician misinterpreted the American Academy of Sleep Medicine's position statement, "the statement merely says that veterans with PTSD should be screened for OSA, that is all, the statement makes no conclusion whatsoever about any causal relationship between PTSD and OSA." The examiner also explained that it was not a study but a questionnaire that was administered in the waiting room of a VA PTSD clinic. The VA examiner stated that there was no attempt to ascertain whether the veterans had OSA. The VA examiner indicated that the private physician's statement was misleading when he stated that there was extensive medical research supporting a direct correlation between PTSD and OSA. The examiner stated that the study indicated that, "the Berlin may be a useful screening tool for OSA".

In May 2021, the Veteran submitted an April 2021 opinion from a private physician. The physician summarized the Veteran's relevant medical records. The physician noted that the Veteran had a sleep evaluation in March 2012, and that the Veteran stated that he was diagnosed with sleep apnea several years earlier but did not follow up to obtain a CPAP. The private physician opined that it is at least as likely as not that the Veteran's OSA clinically developed as a result of his service-connected PTSD. The physician cited several studies, 1.) disturbed sleep associated with military service decreases sleep quality and is suspected to be a common pathway between PTSD and OSA; 2.) chronic stress associated with PTSD has shown to increase the likelihood of developing obstructive sleep apnea and, bidirectionally, sleep disturbances of obstructive sleep apnea increase the likelihood of PTSD; 3.) There are multiple lines of evidence indicating that OSA is more prevalent in psychiatric populations; 4.) Several authors have hypothesized that an association arises because OSA's are often more common during rapid eye movement sleep when decreased tone of airway muscles leads to partial or complete airway obstruction and, consequently, multiple awakening to microarousals from sleep; 5.) The mechanism of dysfunctional REM sleep is the likely reason the two disorders are linked, showing that cohorts of patients with both illnesses have a positive correlation between the percentage of REM sleep and the number of recurrent nightmares 6.) A study found that persons who were adherent to continuous positive airway pressure (CPAP) therapy showed an almost 50% reduction in the frequency of nightmares compared with those who were nonadherent. The physician stated that the September 2019 VA examiner did not correctly analyze the extent of research, but instead described the Veteran's symptoms as strictly associated with obesity. The physician noted that the Veteran had chronic sleep impairments due to PTSD since service and has slowly gained weight. The physician reiterated that the September 2021 VA examiner did not explore the literature, and thus his opinion is misleading. Concluding, the physician opined that the Veteran's OSA at least as likely as not developed as a result of his service-connected PTSD.

The Board considered the Veteran's service treatment records, post-service treatment records, private medical opinions VA medical opinions, and the Veteran's, his spouse, and buddy's lay testimony, and concludes that resolving reasonable doubt in the Veteran's favor that his obstructive sleep apnea is as likely as not proximately due to the Veteran's service-connected PTSD.

The Board acknowledges there are inadequacies in both the

private and VA medical opinions obtained. However, in light of the discussion above, while the evidence is not unequivocal, it has nonetheless placed the record in relative equipoise. Accordingly, the Board finds that element (2) under Allen, nexus, has been satisfied and the appeal for entitlement to service connection for obstructive sleep apnea is granted, as proximately due to his service-connected acquired psychiatric disability.

Citation Nr: A22004725

The Veteran is seeking service connection for the previously denied claim for sleep apnea. The Board finds that new and relevant evidence has been added to the record that warrants readjudication.

The AOJ originally denied the Veteran's claim for service connection for sleep apnea in April 2019. The Veteran did not appeal the decision. Instead, he submitted a Supplemental Claim in August 2019. 38 U.S.C. § 5108; 38 C.F.R. §§ 3.156(d), 3.2501. When a veteran files a Supplemental Claim under the AMA, VA will readjudicate the claim if new and relevant evidenced is presented or secured. 38 U.S.C. § 5108(a); 38 C.F.R. § 3.156(d). New evidence is evidence not previously part of the actual record before agency adjudicators. Relevant evidence is information that tends to prove or disprove a matter at issue in a claim and includes evidence that raises a theory of entitlement that was not previously addressed. 38 C.F.R. § 3.2501(a)(1). The standard shall not be construed to impose a higher evidentiary threshold than the new and material evidence standard that was in effect prior to the date of the enactment of the AMA. See 38 U.S.C. § 5108. If new and relevant evidence is not presented or secured, VA will issue a decision finding that there was insufficient evidence to readjudicate the claim. 38 C.F.R. § 3.2501. The AOJ reconsidered the claim but continued the denial in an October 2019 rating decision.

The Veteran filed another Supplemental Claim in April 2020. He included a positive nexus letter from his private physician. The AOJ denied the claim in April 2020, finding that new and relevant evidence had not been submitted. The evidence reviewed in the April 2020 rating decision appears to include the private medical statement, but it was not discussed in the narrative. Specifically, the AOJ discussed the past Board decisions the Veteran submitted as evidence and his wife's lay statement; however, the AOJ did not address the new and relevant positive nexus opinion.

The Board finds that new evidence was submitted after the prior final rating decision that is relevant to the claim. Specifically, the Veteran's private physician submitted a positive nexus opinion discussing the relationship between his PTSD, obesity, and sleep apnea. The Veteran's claim will be readjudicated in order to address this positive nexus private opinion. Readjudication of the claim for service connection for sleep apnea based on the receipt of new and relevant evidence is therefore warranted. Shade v. Shinseki, 24 Vet. App. 110 (2011) (addressing the nature of the new and material evidence standard; the new and relevant standard is an even lower evidentiary burden).

2. Entitlement to service connection for sleep apnea

The Veteran seeks entitlement to service connection for sleep apnea. He contends that his sleep apnea is secondarily related to his service-connection disabilities. The Veteran has also contended that his sleep apnea is related to his military service as the burn pit exposure during his deployment caused his current respiratory problems. See August 2019 Veteran's Statement in Support of Claim.

Service connection will be granted for disability resulting from disease or injury incurred in or aggravated by active military, naval or air service. 38 U.S.C. § 1110; 38 C.F.R. §

3.303(a). Service connection generally requires evidence of (1) a current disability; (2) lay evidence of in-service incurrence or aggravation of a disease or injury; and (3) a nexus between the claimed in-service disease or injury and the present disability. Shedden v. Principi, 381 F.3d 1163, 1167 (Fed. Cir. 2004); see Caluza v. Brown, 7 Vet. App. 498, 506 (1995).

Service connection may also be established on a secondary basis for disability which is proximately due to, or the result of, a service-connected disability. 38 C.F.R. § 3.310 (a). Secondary service connection may also be established for a disorder which is aggravated by a service-connected disability; compensation may be provided for the degree of disability (but only that degree) over and above the degree of disability existing prior to the aggravation. 38 C.F.R. § 3.310 (b); Allen v. Brown, 8 Vet. App. 374 (1995). To prevail on the issue of secondary service connection, the record must show: (1) evidence of a current disability; (2) evidence of a service-connected disability; and (3) medical nexus evidence establishing a connection between the service-connected disability and the current disability. See Wallin v. West, 11 Vet. App. 509, 512 (1998); see also Allen, 8 Vet. App. 374.

Additionally, VA has established that obesity is not a disability for which service connection can be awarded directly. VA General Counsel Opinion VAOPGCPREC 1-2017 (Jan 6, 2017). Nonetheless, obesity may be an intermittent step between a service-connected disability and a current disability that may be service connected on a secondary basis. To grant service connection, VA would have to resolve the following issues: (1) whether a service-connected disability caused a veteran to become obese; (2) if so, whether the obesity as a result of the service-connected disability was a substantial factor in causing the current disability for which a veteran is seeking service connection; and (3) whether the current disability for which a veteran is seeking service connection would not have occurred but for the obesity caused by the service-connected disability. Id. at 9-10.

Except as otherwise provided by law, a claimant has the responsibility to present and support a claim for benefits. The VA shall consider all information and lay and medical evidence of record in a case and when there is an approximate balance of positive and negative evidence regarding any issue material to the determination of a matter, the VA shall give the benefit of the doubt to the claimant. 38 U.S.C. § 5107; 38 C.F.R. § 3.102.

Turning to the record, in the April 2020 rating decision, the AOJ provided the Favorable Findings that the Veteran is service connected for posttraumatic stress disorder (PTSD), and that he has been diagnosed with sleep apnea. The Board is bound by these favorable findings. 38 C.F.R. § 3.104(c).

The Veteran is also service connected for multiple musculoskeletal disabilities, to include back, left shoulder, knee, hip, ankle, and hand disabilities. The remaining question is whether the Veteran's sleep apnea is related to service or his service-connected disabilities.

The Veteran submitted a disability benefits questionnaire (DBQ) from his private physician in August 2019. The physician confirmed the Veteran's diagnoses of obstructive sleep apnea and periodic limb movement and provided that the Veteran's PTSD is related to his sleep disorders. The physician opined that it is more than likely that the Veteran's sleep apnea is attributable to his PTSD and his active-duty service. He did not provide a rationale to support this opinion and it was not indicated whether the physician reviewed the Veteran's service treatment records (STRs) in conjunction with this opinion. As such, the Board finds this opinion to be inadequate and affords the opinion less probative weight.

The Veteran was afforded a VA examination in October 2019.

The examiner provided a negative nexus opinion with the rationale that sleep apnea is a common disorder in which sleep is disrupted due to an obstruction of airway when throat muscles intermittently relax and block the airway during sleep. The examiner stated that while medical literature supports an increased prevalence of sleep apnea in individuals with major depressive disorder, there has been no evidence or medical literature to conclude that sleep apnea is caused by or secondary to PTSD. The examiner further provided that the claimed disorder of sleep apnea is a separate entity entirely from service-connected PTSD and not the result of it. The examiner did not provide an opinion as to whether the Veteran's sleep apnea is aggravated by his PTSD. The examiner also did not address the Veteran's contention that his sleep apnea is related to in-service exposure to burn pits. As such, the Board finds this opinion to be inadequate and affords the opinion less probative weight.

A private physician's assistant (P.A.) submitted a letter in April 2020. The P.A. noted that she reviewed the Veteran's medical history and personnel records. The Veteran reported difficulty maintaining a meaningful exercise regimen due to his chronic orthopedic pain, which has contributed to significant weight gain. He reported noticing sleep disturbance and daytime fatigue in the early 2010's but did not initially suspect it was due to underlying disease process, he was eventually sent for a sleep study and diagnosed with sleep apnea in 2019. The P.A. provided a positive nexus opinion with the rationale that upon entrance to service the Veteran weighed 170 pounds and he now weighs 225 pounds. The P.A. further provided that the Veteran's weight gain most likely played a role in his sleep disability as his service-connected orthopedic conditions and PTSD contributed greatly to his obesity. Specifically, because of the difficulty in performing strenuous physical exercise or activities due to his service-connected orthopedic conditions and feeling withdrawn from activities he used to get joy out of and avoiding social interactions due to chronic pain and his service-connected PTSD. The Board find the April 2020 provider offered a medical opinion based on her review of the record, available medical literature, and her expertise linking sleep apnea to the Veteran's service-connected disabilities.

The Board finds that the evidence supports a grant of service connection for sleep apnea. The Veteran's VA treatment records show his fluctuation in weight post-service and his difficulty in losing weight to control nonservice-connected disabilities diabetes and hypertension. Additionally, the opinion from the P.A. establishes that the Veteran's service-connected disabilities caused his obesity and his obesity led to him being diagnosed with sleep apnea. The Board finds this opinion to meet all three prongs to establish secondary service connection for sleep apnea secondary to service-connected disabilities through the intermediate step of obesity. As such, service connection for obstructive sleep apnea is granted.

Citation Nr: 22007185

In support of his claim, the Veteran submitted the opinion of a physician that found the Veteran's OSA was at least as likely as not the result of his service-connected PTSD. See March 2017 VA 21-4138 Statement in Support of Claim. By way of rationale, the physician explained that there was a higher prevalence of sleep disorder in patients with psychiatric conditions such as PTSD and there was a higher prevalence of PTSD and hypertension in Veterans. The January 2019 Board remand found this opinion inadequate because correlation is not proof of causation or aggravation and remanded the claim for a VA examination and opinion.

In a November 2021 VA examination, the examiner found that the Veteran's OSA is at least as likely as not to have been aggravated by his service-connected PTSD. By way of rationale, the examiner determined that "disturbed sleep caused by sleep apnea can contribute to sleep deprivation that worsens PTSD symptoms. Even if a sleeper doesn't wake up while experiencing OSA symptoms, sleep apneas arouse the sympathetic nervous system, decreasing overall sleep quality. The resulting sleep deprivation can impair mood and decision-making reducing a person's likelihood of using CPAP therapy, the common treatment for sleep apnea." No other opinions are of record.

The Veteran has a current diagnosis of obstructive sleep apnea, the medical evidence is at least in equipoise that the Veteran's obstructive sleep apnea is proximately due to his service-connected PTSD. Resolving all reasonable doubts in the Veteran's favor, service connection for the Veteran's obstructive sleep apnea is warranted.

Citation Nr: 22017900

In a final November 2018 decision, the Board denied entitlement to service connection for OSA on a direct basis, and therefore this theory of entitlement will not be further addressed herein. The Board has remanded the issue of entitlement to secondary service connection for OSA three timesin November 2018 (for an examination and addendum opinion addressing secondary service connection), July 2020 (for another examination and addendum opinion addressing secondary service connection, as the August 2019 VA opinion was deemed inadequate, as well as updated treatment records), and August 2021. The most recent, August 2021, remand directed provision of updated VA treatment records and an addendum medical opinion regarding obesity as a potential "intermediate step" between the Veteran's service-connected PTSD and his OSA. The examiner was asked to consider and address arguments and medical literature submitted by the Veteran in rendering an opinion.

Upon remand, VA treatment records were updated, and

an addendum medical opinion was secured in September 2021. The AOJ confirmed and continued the prior denial and returned the case to the Board. See September 2021 Supplemental Statement of the Case.

The Veteran asserts that his OSA is "secondary to and/or aggravated by a service-connected psychiatric disorder." See November 3, 2021 Informal Hearing Presentation; October 2013 VA Form 21-0958, Notice of Disagreement. The Board agrees that secondary service connection on a proximate cause basis is warranted, as discussed below.

Secondary service connection may be granted for a disability that is proximately due to or aggravated by a service-connected disability. 38 U.S.C. § 1110, 38 C.F.R. § 3.310.

First, it is undisputed that the Veteran has a current diagnosis of OSA. See, e.g., November 2012 VA Memorandum from Dr. M. Balish ("Your recent sleep study did show sleep apnea."); November 2012 and August 2019 VA examination reports. Moreover, the Veteran has been service-connected for PTSD since November 2011. See October 2012 Rating Decision. Thus, the crux of this case centers on whether OSA is proximately due to or aggravated by service-connected PTSD.

The prior Board remands found the August 2019 and December 2020 VA opinions against the claim to be inadequate.

The latest, September 2021, VA examiner opined that it is less likely than not that the Veteran's OSA is proximately due to or aggravated by his service-connected disability. The Board notes that the August 2021 Remand directed the examiner, in rendering the requested medical opinion(s), to "specifically consider and address" literature submitted by the Veteran, namely:

(i) the July 2011 treatment record by Dr. Bakker noting a

relationship between the Veteran's sleep symptoms and his psychiatric disorder; (ii) the September 2011 VA examination report indicating that the Veteran had a positive history of sleep apnea; (iii) the July 2016 United States House of Representatives Resolution 825 that notes an increased risk of sleep apnea among Soldiers with PTSD; and (iv) the medical articles referenced by the Veteran's representative indicating that Operation Enduring Freedom (OEF)/ Operation Iraqi Freedom (OIF) and Operation New Dawn (OND) veterans with PTSD have been found to be at risk for obstructive sleep apnea at a higher rate compared to those in the community.

The Veteran submitted this literature in support of his argument that an etiological relationship between PTSD and OSA exists, yet, the September 2021 VA examiner failed to address these materials as the August 2021 remand had directed; therefore, the September 2021 opinion is inadequate and non-probative, in addition to all prior opinions of record. See, Stegall v. West, Vet. App. 268 (1998). As the Board has remanded this claim multiple times for an adequate medical opinion but has been unable to obtain one, and there is adequate information to adjudicate the claim, further remand is precluded. See Andrews v. McDonough, 34 Vet. App. 151 (2021).

The Board's synopsized review of the aforementioned literature supports the general proposition that a positive correlation exists between PTSD and OSA among Veterans. In this regard, the 2015 study by Colvonen, et al, is particularly probative, concluding that: "OEF/OIF/OND veterans with PTSD screen as high risk for OSA at much higher rates than those seen in community studies . . . ." Colvonen, et. al., Obstructive Sleep Apnea and Posttraumatic Stress Disorder among OEF/ OIF/OND Veterans [at https:// pubmed.ncbi.nlm.nih.gov/25665698/] (last accessed March 22, 2022). The Board also notes House Resolution 825, recognizing the increased risk of sleep apnea among soldiers with PTSD. The Resolution notes that 54 percent of patients with PTSD who underwent sleep studies at Walter Reed National Military Medical Center were diagnosed with OSA. See H.Res. 825, 114th Congress [available at: https://www.congress.gov/bill/114th-congress/house-resolution/825/text] (last accessed March 22, 2022).

The Board acknowledges that the Veteran did not deploy to a combat theater (OEF/OIF/OND); however, House Resolution 825 supports a relationship between OSA and PTSD, regardless of lack of combat zone service.

Moreover, medical evidence of record also generally supports an etiological relationship between the Veteran's PTSD and his OSA. The Veteran was initially referred to a private sleep medicine clinic during his active service, but the treating physician referred him for a psychiatric evaluation rather than for a sleep study, as the Veteran had expected, which indicates a relationship between his sleep symptoms and his PTSD. See July 2011 Private Treatment Note of K. Bakker, MD; July 2013 Notice of Disagreement. Notably, at that time and in other medical evidence of record, the Veteran reported that his sleep issues began after his in-service trauma. The September 2011 VA general medical examination also notes a positive history for sleep apnea, which is well before the Veteran's separation from service. Moreover, the September 2021 VA PTSD examiner notes OSA as a medical diagnosis relevant to the understanding or management of the Veteran's PTSD, and the November 2020 VA PTSD examiner noted OSA in the "relevant mental health history" section.

Considering that the AOJ has not been able to obtain an adequate nexus opinion, along with the medical treatise evidence submitted by the Veteran (particularly House Resolution 825), the above-cited medical evidence, and the benefit of the doubt doctrine, the Board finds proximate causation is established in this case, and entitlement to secondary service connection for OSA is granted. 38 U.S.C. § 5107; 38 C.F.R. §§ 3.102, 3.310(a).

Citation Nr: A22004134

Service Connection for Obstructive Sleep Apnea, as Secondary to Service Connected PTSD, is Granted

Service connection may be granted for disability arising from disease or injury incurred in or aggravated by active service. 38 U.S.C. § 1110; 38 C.F.R. § 3.303(a). Service connection may be granted for any disease diagnosed after discharge, when all the evidence, including that pertinent to service, establishes that the disease was incurred in service. 38 C.F.R. § 3.303(d). As a general matter, service connection for a disability requires evidence of: (1) the existence of a current disability; (2) the existence of the disease or injury in service, and; (3) a relationship or nexus between the current disability and any injury or disease during service.

Service connection may be granted for disability that is proximately due to or the result of a service-connected disability. An increase in severity of a non service connected disorder that is proximately due to or the result of a service connected disability, and not due to the natural progress of the non service connected condition, will be service connected. Aggravation will be established by determining the baseline level of severity of the non service connected condition and deducting that baseline level, as well as any increase due to the natural progress of the disease, from the current level. See 38 C.F.R. § 3.310; Allen v. Brown, 7 Vet. App. 439, 448 (1995).

Throughout the course of this appeal, the Veteran has sought service connection for obstructive sleep apnea as secondary to service connected PTSD. At the outset, the Board notes that there is a current diagnosis of obstructive sleep apnea. Such diagnosis can be found in the report from an August 2021 VA sleep apnea examination and elsewhere throughout the record.

Having reviewed all the evidence of record, lay and medical, the Board finds the evidence at least in equipoise on the question of whether the currently diagnosed obstructive sleep apnea was caused by the service-connected PTSD.

During the course of this appeal VA received a private sleep apnea medical opinion dated October 2020. The opinion is approximately 20 pages in length, and provides an extensive discussion of the medical literature, the evidence of record, and the Veteran's specific medical circumstances. Per the opinion report, the private examiner opined that the Veteran's medical data and diagnoses, in combination with multiple scientific and medication studies, confirmed that it was more likely than not that the Veteran's PTSD was the sole cause of the currently diagnosed obstructive sleep apnea. In rendering this opinion, the private examiner explicitly addressed the Veteran's obesity risk factor and opined that the medical literature, when combined with the specific facts and circumstances of this Veteran's case, did not support that this Veteran's obstructive sleep apnea was due to obesity, but rather was due to the service-connected PTSD.

In August 2021, a VA examiner appeared to render a negative secondary service connection opinion; however, the rationale provided appeared to be for a negative direct service connection opinion. The AOJ found this opinion to be inadequate, and asked the VA examiner to review the privately submitted medical evidence and render a new secondary service connection opinion. An addendum medical opinion was received in September 2021. Per the opinion report, the VA examiner noted that the privately submitted evidence showed that some medical studies do support that PTSD can affect obstructive sleep apnea. The VA examiner then appears to opine that, based upon this medical literature, the Veteran's sleep apnea was likely caused or aggravated by the service-connected PTSD.

A negative VA secondary service-connection opinion was also received in January 2021. Without commenting on the adequacy of this opinion, the Board finds it to be outweighed by the positive private and VA secondary service connection opinions discussed above. In particular, the Board finds the October 2020 private opinion report to be of more probative value because the private examiner explicitly discussed the facts and circumstances of this Veteran's case, while the January 2021 VA medical opinion was more broadly based.

For the above reasons, and resolving all reasonable doubt in favor of the Veteran, the Board finds that the criteria for service connection for obstructive sleep apnea, as secondary to service connected PTSD, have been met. 38 U.S.C. § 5107(b); 38 C.F.R. § 3.102.

Citation Nr: A22004486

The question then becomes whether a nexus, or relationship, between the Veteran's current disability and the Veteran's service-connected disability has been shown.

The Veteran submitted an opinion from his private physician (Dr. L.G.) on December 14, 2021 a pulmonologist that is board-certified by the American Board of Internal Medicine, Pulmonary Medicine and the National Board of Medical Examiners. The Veteran's private physician opined that it was at least as likely as not that the Veteran's PTSD caused his obstructive sleep apnea (OSA). The Board notes that Dr. G interviewed the Veteran, reviewed the Veteran's medical history in detail and cited to and discussed multiple medical studies/literature in his submitted opinion. The opinion is timely and within the 90-day evidence window and is therefore available for consideration by the Board. This evidence, however, was not available to the RO at the time of the previous denial. The Veteran's representative did submit a waiver of review of this evidence by the Agency of Original Jurisdiction (AOJ).

According to Dr. G, "it is certainly more than reasonable and at least as likely as not that [the Veteran's] PTSD caused his OSA. Dr. G reviewed and discussed in detail the Veteran's medical history and medical records prior to offering this opinion. Dr. G noted that he had considered other risk factors for OSA, such as obesity, being over the age of 40 and hypertension. Dr. G acknowledged that the Veteran was obese with a body mass index (BMI) over 30. However, he noted that the evidence, including the Veteran's sworn statement, demonstrated that the Veteran had sleeping difficulties since his discharge from service. Medical research has found that sleeping impairments lead to physiological, hormonal and behavioral changes that increase the risk for obesity. Of particular interest is the increase in cortisol in response to stress and sleeping difficulties as seen in patients with PTSD. It was further noted that the Veteran was treated at times with Zoloft and Paxil medications for which a known common side effect is weight gain. These medications, in conjunction with the sedentary symptoms of PTSD, led to weight gain thereby further increasing the Veteran's risk of developing OSA. Therefore, Dr. G indicated that the Veteran's PTSD at least contributed to his obese condition, if not caused it.

The record contains no conflicting medical opinion. A review of the evidence of record fails to reflect that the Veteran has been afforded a VA examination regarding this condition and its potential etiology. Therefore, the only substantive evidence of record is that provided by Dr. G. The Board finds this opinion to be highly probative in that it was based on an accurate reporting of the Veteran's medical history with extensive supporting rationale including a thorough discussion of medical studies and literature.

As a final note, the Board recognizes that obesity is not considered a disease or injury for purposes of 38 U.S.C. § 1110 and 1131, and therefore may not be service-connected on a direct basis. See VAOPGCPREC 1-2017. It is possible, however, for obesity to serve as an intermediate step between a service-connected disability and a present disability for the purposes of secondary service connection. See, e.g., VAOPGCPREC 1-2017; 38 C.F.R. § 3.310(a). Under 38 C.F.R. § 3.310(a), a disability which is proximately due to or the result of a service-connected disease or injury is service-connected. When there are potentially multiple causes of a harm, an action is considered to be a proximate cause of the harm if it is a substantial factor in bringing about the harm and the harm would not have occurred but for the action. See VAOPGCPREC 1-2017; see also Walsh v. Wilkie, 32 Vet. App. 300, 306-07 (2020) (holding that obesity can be an "intermediate step" in a causal chain and service connection can be established on either a causal or aggravation basis).

As the weight of the evidence is in favor of the claim of entitlement to service connection for obstructive sleep apnea as secondary to service-connected PTSD, the claim is granted.

Citation Nr: 22018116

Service treatment records (STRs) do not indicate a diagnosis of sleep apnea while the Veteran was in a period of active duty. They do show that a line of duty determination was sought for OSA as a National Guard member. This was initially endorsed by his local command in February 2015, with the finding that the Veteran had difficulty sleeping due to service-connected PTSD, and took sleep medication. He was subsequently diagnosed with sleep apnea "due to [mental health] concerns." The state Adjutant General approved this in November 2015, citing a January 2015 statement from the Veteran's doctor that weight was not the cause of the Veteran's sleep apnea, and reasoning no cause other than the mental disorder was present. However, the Federal National Guard Bureau, the overall command, rejected these lower findings and found OSA was not incurred in the line of duty. They cited the lack of actual substantial evidence supporting a positive determination (required by regulation), and contrary evidence showing an increase in body mass index (BMI) and counseling by medical professionals to lose weight.

The Veteran receives private medical treatment and medical treatment through the VA. The Veteran's medical records indicate that since being diagnosed with sleep apnea he continues to be treated for it with a breathing machine and medication. In his September 2021 hearing, the Veteran testified that he began to have difficulty sleeping (falling and staying asleep) while deployed to Afghanistan in 2013. The Veteran testified that he sought medical treatment while deployed and was given a sleep medication to help him rest in connection with his mental health problems, but he was still fatigued during the day. Upon return from deployment, he testified that he requested a sleep study from his doctor after his wife told him that he was gasping for air in his sleep and snoring more than was usual pre-deployment.

In October 2016, the Veteran's wife submitted a statement that the Veteran rarely snored before his 2013 deployment to Afghanistan, but that upon returning he snored every night and she would hear him stop breathing while he slept. She stated that before he was prescribed a breathing machine, she would sleep on the couch many nights.

In August 2014, the Veteran underwent a sleep study, specifically an overnight polysomnography. The Veteran reported that he has PTSD and his sleep difficulties have worsened since deployment. The Veteran reported daytime fatigue, daily napping after work, feeling drowsy while driving, and trouble with memory and concentration. The Veteran's BMI was recorded at 29. On examination, the Veteran has micrognathia and retrognathia. Post-study, the Veteran reported he slept for 7 hours, did not remember dreaming, and felt sleepy in the morning. Intermittent, mild audible snoring was noted during the study. The Veteran was diagnosed with mild OSA with mild desaturations. OSA was seen exclusively during supine sleep, which constituted half of the total sleep time; OSA was in the severe range during supine sleep. The doctor recommended nasal CPAP titration PSG. The doctor also recommended further investigation to rule out REM sleep behavior disorder. Later in August the Veteran underwent another sleep study after receiving a BiPAP as the Veteran was intolerant of a CPAP. The doctor reported "nearly complete abolishment of apneas, hypopneas, desaturations and snoring... sleep efficiency was excellent." The Veteran's diagnosis was listed as obstructive sleep apnea.

In August 2014, the Veteran was afforded a VA sleep apnea examination. The Veteran reported experiencing persistent daytime hypersomnolence and that his bed partner witnessed apnea versus hypopnea. The Veteran reported receiving a breathing machine the prior week, but that he feels "too much pressure" and "rips" the mask off. The examiner stated that he reviewed the August 2014 sleep study. The Veteran was diagnosed with mild obstructive sleep apnea with Mallampati score Class III-VI. The examiner did not offer any conclusions or opinions on whether the Veteran's sleep apnea was likely due to service.

In January 2015, at a follow up visit for sleep apnea treatment, the Veteran's doctor stated the Veteran's "sleep apnea is not because of his BMI which is not excessive to begin with. His sleep apnea is caused purely by his craniofacial structure, his micrognathia and retrognathia." It was this note that was cited by the investigating officer in the line of duty determination.

In June 2019, a VA opinion by the same examiner as the August 2014 exam concluded that the Veteran's obstructive sleep apnea is not caused by the Veteran's PTSD. The examiner cited several medical articles that suggested OSA may aggravate PTSD symptoms, but OSA is not caused by PTSD. This exam is inadequate because the examiner did not discuss whether OSA is aggravated by PTSD.

In October 2021, the Veteran's representative submitted a positive, private nexus opinion by Dr. V.Z., who is licensed and certified in neurology and sleep medicine. The examiner stated that she reviewed the Veteran's military records, post-service treatment records, VA decisions, and lay statements. The examiner cited much of the Veteran's medical records to support her conclusion that "it is at least as likely as not that his service-connected PTSD led to the development of his OSA, and that his service-connected orthopedic condition and PTSD contributed to the development of his OSA through weight gain." Dr. V.Z. also cited numerous medical studies and articles that show a correlation between PTSD and OSA. The Board notes, however, that correlation is not causation.

Additionally, the Board is aware of peer-reviewed studies that show the potential neurochemical effects of PTSD on sleep apnea and indicate a likelihood that PTSD can cause or aggravate sleep apnea by altering the chemical controllers of the musculature of the throat. See, e.g., Leszek Kubin, Neural Control of the Upper Airway: Respiratory and State-Dependent Mechanisms. Compr. Physiol. vol. 6, 4, 1801-1850 (15 Sep. 2016); Rajesh Kumar, Neural Alterations Associated with Anxiety Symptoms in Obstructive Sleep Apnea Syndrome. Depress. Anxiety vol. 26, 5, 480-91 (2009). Both studies are readily available through the National Library of Medicine (https://www.nlm.nih.gov/).

Given that awareness, the relevancy of the studies, the governmental aspect of availability, and the reasonableness of locating such, the Board finds the studies to be constructively of record. See Euzebio, 989 F.3d 1305, 1321-22 (Fed. Cir. 2021). As the VA medical opinion is not adequate and has little probative value, the medical evidence of record, actual and constructive, must be found to support the claim.

Furthermore, both the Veteran's statements and his wife's statements regarding the onset of his sleep apnea symptoms are competent and consistent. Their descriptions of gasping for breath in his sleep and snoring, including its onset and continuity, are not the type of statements that would require specialized knowledge to perceive or understand. Jandreau v. Nicholson, 492 F.3d 1372 (Fed. Cir. 2007). Consequently, the Board finds the Veteran and his wife's statements persuasive and highly probative.

Though the Board could remand this case again for a new opinion, when considering the Veteran's PTSD and the credible statements of the Veteran and the Veteran's wife regarding his snoring, in combination with the known literature regarding causation, the Board finds that it is reasonable to conclude that the evidence supports the Veteran's claim. The Board will resolve the benefit of the doubt in favor of the Veteran and find that service connection is warranted for OSA. 38 U.S.C. § 5107 (b); 38 C.F.R. § 3.102.

Citation Nr: A22000066

2. Entitlement to service connection for obstructive sleep apnea, to include as secondary to service-connected acquired psychiatric condition is granted.

The Veteran contends that he has sleep apnea secondary to his service-connected psychiatric disorder, to include PTSD and UDD.

As outlined above, service connection may be granted for a disability resulting from a disease or injury incurred in or aggravated by active service. See 38 U.S.C. § 1131; 38 C.F.R. § 3.303. A veteran seeking compensation under these provisions must establish three elements: "(1) the existence of a present disability; (2) in-service incurrence or aggravation of a disease or injury; and (3) a causal relationship between the present disability and the disease or injury incurred or aggravated during service." Saunders v. Wilkie, 886 F.3d 1356, 1361 (Fed. Cir. 2018) (quoting Shedden v. Principi, 381 F.3d 1163, 1167 (Fed. Cir. 2004)).

Service connection may also be granted for a disability that is proximately due to, or aggravated by, service-connected disease or injury. See 38 C.F.R. § 3.310.

The evidence confirms a current diagnosis. Sleep apnea was diagnosed at a sleep study in 2014 and February 2021 VA examination.

The private August 2021 opinion concluded that it is as likely as not that the Veteran's unspecified depressive disorder aided in the development of and permanently aggravated his sleep apnea. This examiner gave a cogent explanation with citation to multiple medical studies supporting this opinion.

The Board acknowledges the February 2021 negative VA opinion finding the Veteran's sleep apnea unrelated to the Veteran's service-connected lung condition; however, the examiner failed to provide an aggravation opinion making this opinion inadequate.

As the February 2021 VA opinion is inadequate, the Board finds that the Veteran's obstructive sleep apnea was caused by the now service-connected psychiatric condition as opined by the August 2021 private physician. As such, service connection for obstructive sleep apnea is warranted on a secondary basis.

Citation Nr: 22020880

1. Entitlement to service connection for sleep apnea, as secondary to PTSD with TBI, is granted.

The Veteran asserts that his sleep apnea is due to his service-connected disabilities, including his PTSD and/or TBI. See, e.g., Board Hearing Transcript. The Board agrees.

Service connection may be granted for a disability resulting from a disease or injury incurred in or aggravated by active service. 38 U.S.C. §§ 1110, 1131; 38 C.F.R. § 3.303.

Secondary service connection may be granted for a disability that is proximately due to or aggravated by a service-connected disability. 38 U.S.C. §§ 1110, 1131; 38 C.F.R. § 3.310.

The Veteran has been diagnosed with sleep apnea and he is in receipt of service connection for TBI and PTSD, among other disabilities. Thus, the key question in this appeal is whether there is an etiological relationship between his current sleep apnea and his TBI.

The evidence against the claim includes the opinion of a VA examiner. The evidence in favor of the claim includes medical opinions and supplemental opinions that the Veteran submitted.

Initially, the Board observes that the VA examiner's opinion did not adequately address secondary service connection due to aggravation. However, remand to correct this deficiency is unnecessary as the record supports the award of secondary service connection on the more favorable proximate cause basis.

The VA examiner diagnosed the Veteran with obstructive sleep apnea and opined that sleep apnea was less likely than not proximately due to or the result of the Veteran's service-connected disabilities. The examiner explained that the pathogenesis of obstructive sleep apnea is not completely understood and noted risk factors for sleep apnea. The examiner acknowledged studies suggesting an association between obstructive sleep apnea and PTSD, as well as TBI, but stated that association does not necessarily establish causation. The examiner explained that "at this time, to my knowledge, the current medical literature does not firmly establish either PTSD or TBI, to be a true disease determinant, rather than merely an associated factor." See September 2016 Sleep Apnea Disability Benefits Questionnaire (DBQ) and Medical Opinion.

Furthermore, the examiner also explained that while medications may exacerbate obstructive sleep apnea, a causative link has not been established. The examiner also explained that the Veteran's sleep disturbances are likely not solely attributed to obstructive sleep apnea, as sleep disturbances also occur with increased frequency in patients with TBI compared to the general population, and as sleep-related breathing disorders are common in patients such as the Veteran who have had a stroke or transient ischemic attack. See id.

In favor of the claim are opinions that the Veteran submitted. The Veteran submitted a medical opinion from Dr. H.G.B., who opined that the Veteran's sleep apnea was directly caused by this depression and PTSD, which in turn were caused by his TBI. See March 2014 H.G.B. Opinion. The Veteran also submitted an opinion from Dr. C.N.B., who stated that literature reports a potential association between sleep apnea and TBI. See December 2013 C.N.B. Opinion. He also submitted an opinion from Dr. H.W.L., who listed sleep apnea among the disabilities that should be service connected. See March 2014 Dr. H.W.L. Report. While these detailed opinions adequately address other disabilities, with respect to sleep apnea they are speculative or lack a rationale and are not probative.

The Veteran subsequently submitted an addendum opinion from Dr. H.W.L. This addendum opinion included a thorough rationale and addressed the opinion of the VA examiner. Dr. H.W.L. noted that the VA examiner's opinion addressed the causes of sleep apnea in generalities but did not focus on the specifics of the Veteran's sleep apnea. He explained that the Veteran was not obese and did not have a compromised upper airway, which are among the risk factors for sleep apnea. Moreover, he explained that the Veteran's sleep apnea was best classified as a "mixed" sleep apnea and stated that this type of sleep apnea was commonly due to a central nervous system disease such as PTSD or TBI. Dr. H.W.L. See January 2018 Dr. H.W.L. Addendum Opinion.

Here, the most probative evidence of record is Dr. H.W.L.'s addendum opinion. In this regard, both Dr. H.W.L. and the VA examiner are competent to provide a medical opinion. However, Dr. H.W.L. is shown to have additional relevant expertise as he is Board certified in sleep medicine. Moreover, Dr. H.W.L.'s opinion focuses on the specifics of the Veteran's appeal. Critically, the VA examiner's opinion indicates that the examiner was not prepared to offer a positive opinion in the absence of literature "firmly establish[ing] either PTSD or TBI as a true disease determinant" or sleep apnea. This requirement for definitive medical evidence demands a higher burden of proof than is required under the Veterans Benefits system. See, e.g., Trimble v. McDonough, No. 21-0843, 2022 U.S. App. Vet. Claims LEXIS 418 (March 25, 2022) (an examiner's opinion based solely on the lack of scientific consensus is improper).

The Board acknowledges that the December 2012 polysomnography report diagnoses the Veteran with obstructive sleep apnea and does not indicate mixed or central sleep apnea. However, the Board interprets Dr. H.W.L.'s description of the Veteran's sleep apnea as "central" or "mixed" as evidencing his opinion that the Veteran's sleep apnea has a component arising from central nervous system. Moreover, the December 2012 polysomnography report affirms the presence of evidence of obstructive sleep apnea and notes that if narcolepsy is a consideration, a repeat study with a multiple sleep latency test should be considered, indicating that the diagnosis of obstructive sleep apnea is not to the exclusion of other diagnoses. See December 2012 Polysomnography Report.

Finally, the Board acknowledges that the Veteran indicated on his substantive appeal that he wished for narcolepsy to be considered as part of his appeal. See January 2017 VA Form 9. The evidence of record does not show a current diagnosis of narcolepsy. See November 2016 Narcolepsy DBQ. However, as noted above, the Board is granting service connection for the Veteran's claimed condition. If the Veteran wishes to seek service connection for an additional sleep condition, he may file a claim on the appropriate VA form.

Citation Nr: 22024999

Service Connection for Sleep Apnea

As indicated above in the Conclusions of Law section, the Board finds that entitlement to service connection for sleep apnea is warranted as secondary to his service-connected asthma and PTSD. Accordingly, the Board grants the Veteran's claim on a secondary basis. 38 C.F.R. § 3.310.

In support of this determination, the Board first notes that, generally, establishing service connection requires competent evidence of: (1) a current disability; (2) an in-service precipitating disease, injury, or event; and (3) a causal relationship, i.e., a nexus, between the current disability and the in-service event. 38 C.F.R. § 3.303 (a); Fagan v. Shinseki, 573 F.3d 1282, 1287 (Fed. Cir. 2009).

Additionally, service connection may also be established for a disability that is proximately due to or the result of a service-connected disability. 38 C.F.R. § 3.310(a). To substantiate secondary service connection, the record must show (1) evidence of a current disability, (2) evidence of a service-connected disability, and (3) medical nexus evidence establishing a connection between the current disability and the service-connected disability. Wallin v. West, 11 Vet. App. 509, 512 (1998); Reiber v. Brown, 7 Vet. App. 513, 516-17 (1995).

Applying these principles to the instant case, the Board finds that the Veteran currently has sleep apnea. Specifically, as documented in a June 2016 VA sleep medicine diagnostic study report, the Veteran was diagnosed with moderate OSA following the performance of sleep study. Accordingly, the Board finds that the first requirement of service connectiona current disabilityhas been satisfied in the instant case.

Next, the Board notes that the Veteran is already service-connected for both asthma and PTSD. Accordingly, pursuant 38 C.F.R. § 3.310, the second requirement of an already service-connected disability has been satisfied.

Lastly, regarding a nexus between the Veteran's current OSA and his service-connected disabilities of asthma and PTSD, the Board first acknowledges that, in December 2021, non-VA provider Dr. Townsend reviewed the Veteran's entire claims file and opined that it was at least as likely as not that the Veteran's OSA was aggravated beyond the normal degree of worsening by PTSD and asthma. In support of this conclusion, Dr. Townsend first explained that it was highly likely that there was a causal relationship between OSA and

PTSD as research had demonstrated that veterans with PTSD had a higher risk of developing sleep apnea. Dr. Townsend then remarked that the Veteran also carried a diagnosis of asthma, and stated that emerging evidence indicated that asthma symptoms, as well as the effects of asthma-controlling medications, could predispose individuals with asthma to OSA. Lastly, Dr. Townsend explained that a recent population-based prospective epidemiological study showed that asthma was associated with an increased risk of new-onset OSA.

The Board finds Dr. Townsend's opinion to be adequate for adjudicative purposes as it was based on a consideration of the Veteran's entire medical history, described the Veteran's condition in detail, and included an explanatory rationale in support of its conclusion. See Stefl v. Nicholson, 21 Vet. App. 120, 124 (2007).

Contrary to Dr. Townsend, in November 2016, a VA clinician opined that the Veteran's sleep apnea was not related to his service-connected PTSD. However, the Board finds this opinion to be of lesser probative value as it did not directly address the concept of aggravation, contrary to the Court of Appeals for Veterans Claims' (Court) holding in Atencio v. O'Rourke, 30 Vet. App. 74, 90 (2018) (holding that, in claims involving service connection on a secondary basis, VA medical opinions must provide separate findings and rationales regarding both causation and aggravation).

Similarly, in January 2020, a VA clinician opined that it was less likely than not that the Veteran's OSA was caused or aggravated by asthma. But, contrary to Atencio, the January 2020 clinician used the same explanatory rationale for both causation and aggravation. Accordingly, the Board finds Dr. Townsend's opinion to be of greater probative value than the November 2016 and January 2020 VA medical opinions.

Lastly, the Board acknowledges that the Veteran was provided another VA medical opinion in May 2019. However, in October 2019, the Board found this opinion to be inadequate and the Board does not disturb this prior finding.

In conclusion, as the evidence of record demonstrates that the Veteran's current OSA was aggravated by his already-service-connected asthma and PTSD, the Board finds that service connection for sleep apnea is warranted. Thus, the Board grants the Veteran's claim. See 38 C.F.R. § 3.310.

Citation Nr: 22014542

1. Entitlement to sleep apnea for obstructive sleep apnea is granted.

The Veteran contends that he has a current diagnosis of obstructive sleep apnea, secondary to his service-connected PTSD, migraines, and a TBI. Alternatively, he contends that his obstructive sleep apnea is directly related to service. See June 2021 Board Hearing Transcript; June 2021 Medical Opinion from A.C. (received July 2021).

Service connection may be established on a secondary basis for a disability that is proximately due to or the result of a service-connected disease or injury. 38 C.F.R. § 3.310 (a). Establishing service connection on a secondary basis requires evidence sufficient to show (1) that a current disability exists and (2) that the current disability was either (a) caused by or (b) aggravated by a service-connected disability. 38 C.F.R. § 3.310 (a); Allen v. Brown, 7 Vet. App. 439 (1995).

The Board notes that, after the Veteran was examined by VA in October 2018, a new sleep study was performed in January 2019. This sleep study indicated the Veteran has a current diagnosis of obstructive sleep apnea. As the October 2018 examiner was not able to consider this examination, the Board finds the October 2018 examination of limited probative value in addressing the Veteran's claim.

Here, the pertinent evidence of record includes a June 2021 positive medical nexus opinion from A.C, a registered nurse. A.C. opined that the Veteran had a number of risk factors that contributed to him developing obstructive sleep apnea, including service-connected PTSD, TBI, and migraine headaches, as well as non-service-connected factors such as genetic predisposition, advanced age, and obesity. A.C. clarified that obstructive sleep apnea is a multifactorial disorder, that the Veteran's service-connected conditions are included in these factors, and that it is not possible to determine, with medical certainty, which risk factor was the primary cause of the Veteran's obstructive sleep apnea. A.C. provided a well-reasoned opinion, illustrating the link between the Veteran's service-connected disabilities and his sleep apnea based on an application of medical literature to the Veteran's case, showing a link between symptoms of the Veteran's service-connected disabilities (such as sleep fragmentation, medication induced changes to breathing, and decreased motivation to exercise) and the Veteran's development of obstructive sleep apnea.

As A.C. has persuasively reasoned that it is not possible to differentiate which of the Veteran's risk factors for obstructive sleep apnea are primarily responsible for his development of sleep apnea, the Board will resolve all doubt in the Veteran's favor and find that the Veteran's sleep apnea is at least as likely as not attributable to his service-connected conditions of PTSD, TBI, and migraine headaches.

Accordingly, after resolving all doubt in favor of the Veteran, the Board finds that service connection for obstructive sleep apnea is warranted. 38 U.S.C. § 5107; 38 C.F.R. § 3.102, 3.310.

Citation Nr: 22023436

In January 2020, the Board remanded this matter for additional development, which has been completed. A remand by the Board confers upon the Veteran, as a matter of law, the right to compliance with remand instructions, and imposes upon VA a concomitant duty to ensure compliance with the terms of the remand. See Stegall v. West, 11 Vet. App. 268, 271 (1998). Where the remand orders of the Board are not complied with, the Board errs as a matter of law when it fails to ensure compliance.

The Board finds that the AOJ did not substantially comply with the January 2020 remand directives. However, upon further review, a complete grant of the benefit sought is warranted, and so the Veteran is not prejudiced by the failure to remand for compliance.

Service connection will be granted if it is shown that the veteran suffers from a disability resulting from personal injury suffered or disease contracted in the line of duty, or for aggravation of a preexisting injury suffered or disease contracted in the line of duty, during active military service. 38 U.S.C. § 1131; 38 C.F.R. § 3.303. Disorders diagnosed after discharge will still be service connected if all the evidence, including that pertinent to service, establishes that the disease was incurred in service. 38 C.F.R. § 3.303(d); see also Combee v. Brown, 34 F.3d 1039, 1043 (Fed. Cir. 1994).

In order to establish service connection on a direct basis, the record must contain competent evidence of: (1) the existence of a present disability; (2) in-service incurrence or aggravation of a disease or injury; and (3) a causal relationship between the present disability and the disease or injury incurred or aggravated during service. Shedden v. Principi, 381 F.3d 1163, 1167 (Fed. Cir. 2004).

Service connection may also be warranted for disability proximately due to or the result of a service-connected disease or injury. 38 C.F.R. § 3.310(a). This permits service connection not only for a disability caused by a service-connected disability, but for the degree of disability resulting from aggravation of a disability by a service-connected disability. See Allen v. Brown, 7 Vet. App. 439, 448 (1995). In the case of aggravation by a service-connected disability, a Veteran may be compensated for the degree of disability over and above the degree of disability existing prior to the aggravation. Id.; see also 38 C.F.R. § 3.310(b).

In determining whether service connection is warranted for a disability, VA is responsible for determining whether the evidence supports the claim or is in relative equipoise, with the veteran prevailing in either event, or whether the evidence is against the claim, in which case the claim is denied. 38 U.S.C. § 5107; Gilbert v. Derwinski, 1 Vet. App. 49 (1990). When there is an approximate balance of evidence regarding any issue material to the determination, the benefit of the doubt is afforded the claimant.

In January 2017, the AOJ obtained an opinion on the etiology of the Veteran's OSA. The 2017 opinion indicated that the claimed condition is less likely than not proximately due to or the result of the Veteran's service-connected condition as "there is no relation between PTSD and sleep apnea. They are entirely distinct and separate entities."

In December 2019, the Veteran's representative submitted an article on sleep and mental health, which indicated a potential link between the development of sleep apnea and the presence of PTSD in Veterans.

In a January 2020 opinion, a VA examiner opined that the Veteran's OSA was less likely than not (less than 50 percent probability) incurred in or caused by the claimed in-service injury, event, or illness. The examiner noted that the Veteran's BMI was 32 when he was diagnosed with sleep apnea in 2016, which was considered obese. The examiner indicated that obesity was the number one cause of OSA. She wrote that sleep studies were the gold standard for the diagnosis of OSA. She explained that the evidence in-service did not show OSA and snoring alone was not indicative of sleep apnea. Therefore, his OSA was not caused or aggravated by his military service. The Board finds the opinion as to direct service connection inadequate. The examiner failed to provide an adequate rationale in relying mainly on the lack of an in-service diagnosis.

An addendum opinion was secured in February 2020; the examiner addressed the article submitted by the Veteran, and stated that such only address correlation, and did not indicate causation. She indicated that PSTD causes chemical changes in the brain, while sleep apnea is related to anatomical changes in the airway. She repeated that the Veteran's reported snoring did not in and of itself show onset in service.

The Board takes notice of Neural Control of the Upper Airway: Respiratory and State-Dependent Mechanisms, Kubin, L., Comprehensive Physiology, 2016 Sep. 15; 6(4), ppg. 1801-1850, and Neural Alterations Associated with Anxiety Symptoms in Obstructive Sleep Apnea Syndrome, Kumar, R., et. al., Depression and Anxiety, 2009; 26(5), ppg. 480-491. The studies addressed statistical correlations between psychiatric disorders and obstructive sleep apnea, and the potential causal linkage attributable between the two due to neurological effects of hyperactivity caused by psychiatric disorders upon throat muscle contraction during sleep and consequently anatomic obstruction. Both studies are readily available through the National Library of Medicine (https://www.nlm.nih.gov/). As such, the studies are constructively before the Board, and were before the AOJ at the time of the decision on appeal. See Euzebio v. McDonough, 989 F.3d 1305, 1321-22 (Fed. Cir. 2021).

These studies directly refute the negative opinion of the 2020 VA examiner. In fact, her statement that PTSD is manifested by chemical changes in the brain would in fact tend to support the conclusions of the studies cited above. The Board therefore finds there is an approximate balance of positive and negative evidence regarding the nexus issue, and the Board will give the benefit of the doubt to the claimant. 38 U.S.C. § 5107(b); see also Gilbert v. Derwinski, 1 Vet. App. 49, 53-54 (1990). In light of the positive and negative evidence of record, to include specifically the VA medical opinions and studies of which are constructively before the Board, the Board finds that the evidence is at least in equipoise regarding whether the Veteran's sleep apnea was caused by his service-connected PTSD. Hence, affording him the benefit of the doubt, service connection for obstructive sleep apnea is warranted.

Citation Nr: 22002870

Obstructive sleep apnea

The Veteran contends that his current obstructive sleep apnea is causally linked to his service-connected PTSD. For the following reasons, the Board agrees that service connection is warranted.

As an initial matter, the Board notes that the Veteran has been diagnosed with obstructive sleep apnea during the pendency of the appeal. His attorney reported at their Board hearing that the Veteran was given a sleep study in 2020 which confirmed the diagnosis; and in July 2021 the Veteran submitted an evaluation from a private psychologist noting that he used a CPAP machine for his sleep apnea. The question at issue is whether there is a causal link between his sleep apnea and his service-connected acquired psychiatric disorder.

In this regard, the positive evidence of record includes an opinion authored by a private psychologist finding that it is likely that the Veteran's PTSD aggravated his sleep apnea.

By way of rationale, the psychologist noted that there is an increased incidence of obstructive sleep apnea and sleep disturbance more generally among veterans with PTSD. He explained that studies showed a number of factors may play a role in the association between psychiatric disorders and sleep apnea. In many cases, for example, psychiatric disorders were shown to increase central nervous system activation and endocrine dysregulation, which could eventually cause further biological dysregulation and metabolic syndrome, resulting in sleep apnea. The psychologist noted that he had reviewed the current credible professional medical literature on the subject and found "the phenomenon of OSA developing from PTSD to be very well described." Moreover, in the psychologist's opinion the Veteran shared many characteristics with the subjects discussed in the literature (for whom there was a causal link between sleep apnea and PTSD). In sum, the psychologist opined that the Veteran's PTSD-related sleep disturbances could at least as likely as not be said to aggravate his obstructive sleep apnea.

The Board acknowledges that the psychologist's opinion could perhaps have been supported by a more thorough explanation. The opinion appears to rely on general studies and principles and lacks detailed analysis connecting the literature to the Veteran's specific case (including his personal symptom history and physical characteristics). Moreover, the evidence of record weighs against a finding of in-service incurrence or that the Veteran's PTSD was the original cause of his obstructive sleep apnea. However, 38 C.F.R. § 3.310 allows for service connection to be granted on the basis of aggravation, and in this regard the psychologist's opinion supports the contention that the Veteran's sleep apnea was aggravated by his PTSD. The Veteran has never been afforded a VA examination in this matter; there is no credible medical evidence calling the private psychologist's opinion into question. The Board is not permitted to ignore or disregard the conclusions of a medical professional, nor to substitute its own judgment on a medical matter. See Colvin v. Derwinski, 1 Vet. App. 171 (1991); Willis v. Derwinski, 1 Vet. App. 66 (1991).

In sum, when resolving all reasonable doubt in the Veteran's favor, the Board finds it is at least as likely as not that his obstructive sleep apnea was aggravated by his service-connected acquired psychiatric disorder, to include PTSD. The claim for service connection will be granted.

Citation Nr: A22000900

The Board notes that the Veteran's service records do not contain any complaints, treatment, or diagnosis for OSA or sleep troubles. The first indication for OSA occurs in September 2006 when he complained of sleep trouble and the clinician stated the Veteran needs a sleep study. No sleep study appears in the Veteran's current record but as noted, subsequent records have diagnosed OSA and, at least by November 2009, the Veteran had been issued a CPAP to treat or alleviate the OSA symptoms. Further, there are no opinions which link the Veteran's OSA directly to service.

Moreover, the Board understands that the Veteran is not contending his OSA is directly related to service. Instead, the Veteran contends that his service-connected PTSD caused or aggravated his OSA. Treatment records, beside noting the OSA treated with a CPAP, also indicate the Veteran's PTSD causes sleep impairment even with CPAP use. Thus, the Board will decide the Veteran's claim based on whether the Veteran's OSA resulted from or aggravated by a service-connected disability including PTSD.

An August 2021 VA examiner concluded that despite the Veteran's use CPAP, the Veteran did not have OSA because of a lack of objective evidence establishing OSA. As noted above, VA has already found the Veteran has a current OSA disability. Therefore, the Board places little probative value on the August 2021 VA examiner's opinion.

The Veteran has submitted the private doctor, Dr. L. Gillard, a pulmonologist, who concluded in an April 2020 opinion that it is at least as likely as not the Veteran's PTSD contributed to the development of OSA. He cited medical literature that found a correlation between OSA and PTSD. In particular, one study noted sleep fragmentation (such as is prevalent in PTSD) increases the propensity for upper airway collapse in patients with sleep apnea. Patients with PTSD have more fragmented sleep, with more awakenings in the first half of the night. Another cited study shows that PTSD patients had a decreased percentage of slow-wave sleep relative to controls, which may explain their increased arousals during the first half of the night. In Dr. Gillard's opinion, the cited research shows a causal effect is likely with a high degree of certainty between the symptoms of PTSD related to sleep deficit and the severity of OSA. The Board notes Dr. Gillard conceded that the Veteran had other risk factors for OSA such as weight, age, gender, hypertension, and diabetes. The Veteran is also service connected for hypertension.

Other than the August 2021 VA examiner's opinion, there are no other significant opinions in conflict with Dr. Gillard's opinion. As noted, the Board finds the August 2021 opinion is not entitled to a probative value because the examiner ignored the Veteran's established OSA diagnosis. Further, the Board finds Dr. Gillard's opinions are well reasoned, detailed, consistent with other evidence of record, included reviews of the claims file and reference to the medical literature. Prejean v. West, 13 Vet. App. 444, 448-49 (2000) (factors for assessing the probative value of a medical opinion are the physician's access to the claims file and the thoroughness and detail of the opinion)

Upon review of the record, the Board finds the evidence to at least be in equipoise as to whether the Veteran's current OSA is proximately due to or aggravated beyond its natural progression by his service-connected PTSD. Accordingly, after resolving all doubt in favor of the Veteran, the Board finds that service connection for OSA is warranted. 38 U.S.C. § 5107; 38 C.F.R. § 3.102.

Citation Nr: 22018229

2. Entitlement to service connection for sleep apnea

The Veteran asserts that he is entitled to service connection for sleep apnea.

The Board concludes that the Veteran has a current disability that is the result of his service-connected PTSD. 38 U.S.C. §§ 1110, 1131; Allen v. Brown, 7 Vet. App. 439 (1995) (en banc); 38 C.F.R. § 3.310(a).

Although service treatment records are silent for any complaints or diagnosis related to a sleep disorder, the Veteran provided testimony about his sleep troubles during service. At the Board hearing, the Veteran explained that because he was a trauma nurse during service, he often self-treated his ailments. He stated that he experienced a lack of sleep due to his shift schedule while serving in Afghanistan, and that he was exhausted during the day due to not sleeping at night. The Veteran indicated that after service discharge, his spouse at the time noticed that he often stopped breathing during sleep.

In September 2015, the Veteran underwent a sleep study and was diagnosed with obstructive sleep apnea. During the same month, the Veteran's primary care VA physician, Dr. J.L., provided a letter stating he has treated the Veteran since March 2015, and is familiar with his service treatment records and post-service medical records. He noted that the Veteran had no known history of sleep apnea prior to his military service. Therefore, he opined that it is more likely than not that the Veteran's sleep apnea originated during service and is also secondary to the Veteran's service-connected PTSD. In December 2017, Dr. J.L. provided another letter in support of the Veteran's claim, again opining that it is more likely than not that his sleep apnea is secondary to service-connected PTSD. Dr. J.L. discussed medical literature and research that determined sleep impairment is a core feature of PTSD.

Accordingly, after resolving all doubt in favor of the Veteran, the Board finds that service connection for sleep apnea as secondary to service-connected PTSD is warranted. 38 U.S.C. § 5107; 38 C.F.R. § 3.102.

Citation Nr: 22002399

The diagnosis was obstructive sleep apnea. The examiner indicated that the Veteran's obstructive sleep apnea was less likely than not (less than 50 percent) proximately due to, or the result of, his PTSD because there was no medical nexus for PTSD to cause obstructive sleep apnea. The examiner reported that the Veteran's obstructive sleep apnea was likely due to his nonservice-connected risk factor of obesity because obesity was a strong risk factor for obstructive sleep apnea, and that Veteran had a body mass index (BMI) of 38 at the time of his sleep apnea diagnosis.

The Board observes that the Veteran's service treatment records do not specifically show treatment for sleep apnea. The Board notes, however, that post-service treatment records show that the Veteran was treated for sleep apnea, including with sleep studies. Additionally, the Board observes that the Veteran has reported that he suffered from sleep apnea symptoms, such as snoring, and interrupted sleep, with waking up without breathing, when he served in Afghanistan. The Board further notes that the Veteran's mother reported that when the Veteran came home from the military, she would hear him snoring, and then the snoring would become quiet, as if he stopped breathing. She maintained that she would call the Veteran from downstairs just to hear him speak, and to start breathing.

The Board observes that a November 2017 VA sleep apnea examination report relates a diagnosis of obstructive sleep apnea. The examiner indicated that the Veteran's obstructive sleep apnea was less likely than not proximately due to, or the result of, his PTSD because there was no medical nexus for PTSD to cause obstructive sleep apnea. The examiner reported that the Veteran's obstructive sleep apnea was likely due to his nonservice-connected risk factor of obesity because obesity was a strong risk factor for obstructive sleep apnea, and that Veteran had a body mass index (BMI) of 38 at the time of his sleep apnea diagnosis. The Board notes that the examiner solely addressed whether the Veteran's sleep apnea was proximately due to, or the result of, his service-connected PTSD, with polysubstance abuse. The Board observes that the examiner did not address whether the Veteran's service-connected PTSD, with polysubstance abuse, aggravated his sleep apnea. In El-Amin v. Shinseki, 26 Vet. App. 136 (2013), a decision issued by the United States Court of Appeals for Veterans Claims (Court), the Court vacated a decision of the Board where a VA examiner did not specifically opine as to whether a disability was aggravated by a service-connected disability.

Additionally, the Board notes that the examiner did not address direct service connection for the Veteran's claimed sleep apnea. The Board further observes that the examiner did not address the Veteran's reports of sleep problems during service and since service. The Board observes that the Veteran is competent to report sleep problems during service and since service. See Davidson, 581 F.3d at 1313. The examiner also did not address the reports by the Veteran's mother that when the Veteran came home from the military, she would hear him snoring, and then the snoring would become quiet, as if he stopped breathing. See Davidson, 581 F.3d at 1313. The Board further notes that the examiner did not address the Veteran's claimed sleep apnea, pursuant to the provisions of 38 C.F.R. § 3.317. Therefore, the Board finds that the opinions provided by the examiner, pursuant to the November 2017 VA sleep apnea examination report, are not probative in this matter.

The Veteran is diagnosed with sleep apnea. The Board finds the Veteran's reports of sleep apnea symptoms during service and since service to be credible. See Jandreau, 492 F.3d at 1372 (holding that lay evidence can be competent and sufficient to establish a diagnosis of a condition when a lay person is competent to identify the medical condition, or reporting a contemporaneous medical diagnosis, or the lay testimony describing symptoms at the time supports a later diagnosis by a medical professional). The Board also finds that the reports from the Veteran's mother that when the Veteran came home from the military, she would hear him snoring, and then the snoring would become quiet, as if he stopped breathing, to be credible.

Resolving any doubt in the Veteran's favor, the Board finds that the evidence is at least in equipoise regarding whether his current sleep apnea commenced during his period of service. In light of the evidence, the Board cannot conclude that the preponderance of the evidence is against granting service connection for sleep apnea. Therefore, service connection for sleep apnea, is warranted. See 38 U.S.C. § 5107 (b); 38 C.F.R. § 3.102. As the Board has granted direct service connection in this matter, it need not address other theories of service connection.

Citation Nr: 22013919

The Veteran contends that his sleep apnea was caused by his

service-connected PTSD.

The Veteran underwent a VA examination in December 2019. The examiner ultimately concluded that it was less likely than not that the Veteran's sleep apnea was proximately due to the Veteran's PTSD. However, as noted in the June 2021 JMPR, this opinion failed to discuss whether the Veteran's OSA was aggravated by the Veteran's service-connected PTSD. Therefore, it is inadequate for adjudication purposes.

The Veteran provided a November 2021 private medical opinion. This opinion stated that it was more likely than not that the Veteran's sleep apnea is due to his PTSD. Specifically, the physician noted that it is well known that PTSD can contribute to the development of OSA and exacerbate its symptoms. Further the physician stated that there is robust medical literature showing PTSD triggered sleep fragmentation and promoting upper airway collapsibility, the hallmark of OSA's pathology. The physician ultimately concluded that this data, combined with the Veteran's documented hypervariability and characteristic CPAP mask claustrophobia, illustrates the Veteran's OSA is secondary to his PTSD.

The Board finds the evidence to be in relative equipoise. If the evidence is supportive or is in relative equipoise, then the Veteran prevails. See 38 C.F.R. § 3.102. Accordingly, service connection for sleep apnea is granted. 38 C.F.R. § 3.303(b).

Citation Nr: 22024771

As to a current diagnosis, the Board notes that the Veteran's disability has been diagnosed as obstructive sleep apnea.

As to the Veteran's contentions, the Board notes that the Veteran has asserted that his disability is related to his service in Afghanistan or his service-connected PTSD.

As to the in-service incurrence, the Board notes that

the Veteran's service treatment records are silent for any treatment or a diagnosis for sleep apnea. However, the records do reflect significant weight gain during service as demonstrated by weight in pounds of 188 in March 2002, 180 in May 2002, 194 in July 2003, 182 in August 2003, 264 in October 2010, and 260 in April 2011. Post service, the Veteran's weight was noted as 305 in September 2014, approximately one year following the Veteran's discharge from active service.

Turning to the medical opinion evidence at hand, the Board notes that the Veteran attended a VA examination for this issue in February 2020. Following the examination, the examiner found that the Veteran's disability was less likely as not related to his military service or his service-connected PTSD. The examiner stated that the major risk factors for OSAHS are obesity and male sex. The examiner stated that additional risk factors include mandibular retrognathia and micrognathia, a positive family history of OSAHS, genetic syndromes that reduce upper airway patency (e.g., Down syndrome, Treacher-Collins syndrome), adenotonsillar hypertrophy (especially in children), menopause (in women), and various endocrine syndromes (e.g., acromegaly, hypothyroidism). The examiner stated that approximately 40-60 percent of cases of OSAHS are attributable to excess weight. The examiner stated that the prevalence of OSAHS is two to fourfold higher among men than among women. The examiner stated that notably, PTSD is not a recognized cause of, or risk factor for OSA. The examiner stated that this veteran is obese, with a weight of 330 pounds and a BMI of 46. The examiner stated that while some studies suggest a correlation of PTSD and OSA, it is important to note that correlation does not necessarily mean causation. The examiner stated that "the assumption that A causes B simply because A correlates with B is a logical fallacy-it is not a legitimate form of argument. Correlation must always be put into perspective." The examiner stated that the weakness of observational studies is that all of the variables cannot be controlled for. The examiner stated that researchers can account for known variables (e.g. race, age, and sex), but it is always the unknown variables that can confound such studies. The examiner stated that correlation alone cannot be used as evidence for a cause-and-effect relationship between a risk factor and a disease. The examiner stated that it is one of the most abused types of evidence, because it is easy and even tempting to come to premature conclusions based upon the preliminary appearance of a correlation. The examiner stated that in my opinion "it is less likely than not that this Veteran's OSA was caused or aggravated by the SC PTSD, because of the lack of a known pathophysiologic relationship, the inherent weakness of observational studies, the lack of clear and convincing evidence of causation, and the fact that this Veteran has the following well-defined risk factors for OSA: male gender, obesity (BMI 46), upper airway soft-tissue abnormalities (Mallampati 34, neck circ 18, nasal congestion)." The examiner stated that these well-defined risk factors are by far the most likely etiology of his OSA. The examiner stated that therefore, in my opinion, it is less likely than not that this Veteran's OSA is secondary to his SC conditions listed above.

The Board acknowledges that the Veteran's representative cited to medical journal articles that discussed PTSD and sleep apnea. The Board is unable to place any probative value on this information because these articles are not accompanied by a medical opinion and these articles do not address the facts that are specific to the Veteran's case.

The Board has also reviewed the Veteran's medical treatment records. The Board finds that the Veteran's records are silent for a medical opinion that has found that the Veteran's disability is related to his military service or his service-connected PTSD. However, notwithstanding the fact that the February 2020 VA examiner did not find that Veteran's sleep apnea was related to his service or service-connected disability, the examiner did find that the most significant cause of sleep apnea was obesity, and while the examiner did acknowledge the Veteran's then-current weight of 330 pounds, the examiner did not address the Veteran's weight gain from early in his military career of 180 pounds that later was noted to be as mush as 264 pounds in October 2010. Consequently, based on the examiner's own opinion and a more comprehensive review of the record, the Board will give the Veteran's significant weight gain during service of as much as 84 pounds contributed to his sleep apnea, and that service connection for sleep apnea is therefore warranted.

Citation Nr: 22016361

A July 2021 private medical consultation based on a record review has been obtained regarding the Veteran's sleep apnea (10/22/2021 Medical Treatment Record - Non-Government Facility). The private physician opined it is more likely than not that the Veteran's sleep apnea is a direct complication of his PTSD, caused by his active service (10/22/2021 Medical Treatment Record - Non-Government Facility, pg. 2).

The practitioner's opinion includes consideration of and citation to medical journal articles and reflects familiarity with the Veteran's medical and service history. As such, the Board finds the opinion highly probative, weighing in favor of the Veteran's claim.

Finding the weight of the most probative evidence of record to be in favor of the Veteran's claim, the Board finds entitlement to service connection for sleep apnea, to include as proximately due to service-connected PTSD, is warranted.

Citation Nr: 22005947

The Veteran asserts that his OSA is due to his service-connected PTSD. Post-service treatment records show the Veteran has been diagnosed with OSA and PTSD. The Veteran is service connected for PTSD. Thus, the question before the Board is whether the Veteran's service-connected PTSD caused or aggravated the Veteran's OSA.

The Veteran was afforded a VA opinion in May 2015. The examiner ultimately opined that it was less likely than not that the Veteran's sleep apnea is secondary to his PTSD. The examiner wrote the Veteran was diagnosed with sleep apnea in 2004 when his BMI (Body Mass Index) was 35 and defined as obese. The examiner went on to state that the most significant risk factors for sleep apnea are age, obesity, and male gender. Additionally, the examiner wrote that the Veteran was on no medication to treat his PTSD which might have either contributed to his obesity or to decreased central respiratory drive.

The Board finds the May 2015 VA opinion inadequate and holds little probative value. See Barr v. Nicholson, 21 Vet. App. 303, 312 (2007) (holding that when VA undertakes to provide a VA examination or obtain a VA opinion, it must ensure that the examination or opinion is adequate). Although the May 2015 examiner provided a nexus opinion, the examiner did not opine of whether the Veteran's PTSD aggravated the Veteran's OSA. Additionally, the VA examiner mentioned that the Veteran's PTSD could have contributed to his obesity, which the examiner listed as a substantial risk factor for OSA.

In July 2015, the Veteran submitted an opinion from Dr. R.H. dated July 3, 2015. Dr. R.H. stated that the Veteran has been under his care since May 2013. Dr. R.H. cited multiple studies regarding the link between PTSD and OSA and described how the symptoms of insomnia and sleep apnea are related to PTSD. Dr. R.H. opined that the Veteran is severely affected by sleep apnea and is secondary to his PTSD.

In November 2017, the Veteran submitted a private medical opinion by Dr. I.B. dated November 9, 2017. Dr. I.B. wrote that peer reviewed journals indicate that there is link between PTSD and OSA. More importantly, Dr. I.B. opined that the Veteran's sleep apnea is secondary to his PTSD and is more likely than not a result of his military service.

In August 2021, the Veteran submitted a letter from Dr. E.F. dated May 28, 2021. Dr. E.F. confirmed the Veteran's diagnoses for OSA and PTSD. Dr. E.F. went on to opine that he believes that PTSD is causing OSA. Dr. E.F. wrote the Veteran is like many of his combat veterans and that he has progressed from insomnia and nightmares to OSA.

As the Board finds the VA opinion regarding secondary service connection inadequate, there is no other competent VA medical opinion of record addressing secondary service connection. However, the Veteran has submitted multiple opinions in support of his claim. Additionally, the Veteran has submitted scientific studies himself and as part of his private opinion. As the Board finds the medical opinions submitted by the Veteran as competent and probative in addressing whether OSA is caused by a service-connected disability, the Board finds the preponderance of the evidence supports a finding that his OSA is caused by his service-connected PTSD. Therefore, service connection for OSA is warranted.

Citation Nr: A22006107

1. Entitlement to service connection for obstructive sleep apnea (OSA), to include as secondary to service-connected disabilities

The Veteran contends that he suffers from OSA associated with his service-connected conditions. Specifically, the Veteran contends his OSA condition developed as a result of his obesity, which is attributable to his mental health condition and painful physical disabilities.

The Board establishes the Veteran has a current diagnosis of OSA. Further, the Board acknowledges the Veteran is service-connected for his PTSD, bilateral pes planus, and bilateral shoulder disabilities. Thus, the issue of the Veteran's claim for service connection turns on whether the evidence of record demonstrates the Veteran's OSA was either caused or aggravated by the Veteran's service-connected PTSD. Here, the Board concludes the evidence of record supports such a finding.

The Veteran's VA medical records include a diagnosis of OSA in a May 2011 VA sleep study.

The record contains the Veteran's March 2017 private sleep apnea disability benefits questionnaire. The private physician confirmed the Veteran's diagnosis of OSA with a prescribed CPAP machine. The private physician noted the Veteran's progressive weight gain and present obesity. The examiner noted the Veteran's current formal diagnosis of PTSD involved documented symptomatology, including depressive mood, intermittent anxiety, and associated sleep disturbance. The examiner noted medical literature, which reported the established documented association in the veteran population that PTSD leads to weight gain with a strong propensity for obesity related to an associated metabolic dysfunction. Additionally, the private examiner cited to studies within medical literature that reported chronic partial sleep loss increased the risk of obesity and weight gain. The examiner cited to a medical study that found obesity is associated with mood, anxiety, and somatoform disorders as well as elevations in psychological distress. Further, the Veteran's private physician noted that multiple studies documented obesity as a high-risk factor for OSA. Finally, the Veteran's private physician provided the medical opinion that it is more likely than not that the Veteran's OSA condition is secondary to, related to, and/or aggravated by his service-connected PTSD with associated sleep disturbance, decreased activity, weight gain, and obesity.

In June 2017, the Veteran underwent a VA examination to address the Veteran's OSA. The VA examiner confirmed the Veteran's diagnosis of OSA. The VA examiner provided the medical opinion that the Veteran's OSA was less likely than not proximately due to or the result of the Veteran's service-connected disabilities. The VA examiner opined that sleep apnea is due to an obstructed airway causing pauses in breathing and snoring. It is not directly caused by PTSD.

VA provided another medical opinion regarding the Veteran's OSA in September 2020. The VA medical examiner provided the opinion that the Veteran's OSA was less likely than not proximately due to of the result of the Veteran's service-connected condition. The VA examine stated medical literature did not support that PTSD causes sleep apnea, as PTSD does not cause a physical obstruction in the airway.

In October 2020 and November 2020, the RO provided the Veteran a VA medical opinion disability benefits questionnaire and subsequent addendum medical opinion. The VA examiners confirmed the Veteran's diagnosis of an OSA condition. The VA examiners provided the medical opinions that the Veteran's OSA was less likely than not proximately due to or the result of the Veteran's service-connected disabilities, to include as related to the Veteran's weight gain and obesity. The October 2020 VA examiner reported that it was less likely than not that the Veteran's service-connected disabilities caused the Veteran to become obese. The VA clinician opined that, while mental health conditions such as PTSD can impact motivation and can lead to overeating, there are strategies to prevent obesity. Further the November

2020 VA examiner opined that the Veteran's service-connected conditions did not preclude all forms of exercise, and therefore the examiner could not say the Veteran's service-connected disabilities were substantial factors to OSA. Additionally, the VA examiner stated that she could not state without mere speculation whether the Veteran's OSA would not have started but for obesity.

Notably, the VA examiners did not provide a medical opinion as to aggravation between OSA and the Veteran's service-connected musculoskeletal disorders and PTSD.

The Veteran submitted a medical opinion from his VA treating physician in June 2020. The Veteran's VA physician provided the opinion that the Veteran's OSA was secondarily related to his primary rated disabilities. The VA physician noted the Veteran's musculoskeletal conditions and his psychiatric disorders caused the Veteran's Body Mass Index (BMI) to rise above 30, indicating obesity. The physician stated the Veteran's OSA was related to obesity.

The Veteran testified before the Board in November 2021. The Veteran testified he experienced pain from his service-connected shoulder, feet, and back disorders, which caused him to avoid exercise. The Veteran also noted his symptoms of depression affected his motivation to get up and do activities. The Veteran reported that he gained weight and did not want to exercise.

In November 2021, the Veteran submitted an additional private sleep apnea disability benefits questionnaire. Following a review of the Veteran's records, the private clinician confirmed the Veteran's diagnosis of OSA. The private physician provided the medical opinion that the Veteran's diagnosis of OSA was secondarily related to his primary rated disability of PTSD and musculoskeletal conditions. The private physician opined that the Veteran's

OSA was due to the Veteran's symptoms of depression and associated side-effects of pharmaceutical drugs used to treat the Veteran's PTSD, which caused the Veteran's undesired weight gain. The examiner noted the Veteran's depressive symptoms led to poor eating habits, including increased amounts of food and unhealthy choices leading to obesity. The examiner noted the Veteran's obesity was a risk factor to OSA.

The Board finds that the criteria for service connection for sleep apnea secondary to the Veteran's PTSD have been met. The record shows that the Veteran has a current diagnosis of sleep apnea, and there is competent evidence that the current disability was either caused or aggravated by a service-connected disability. Here, the Board finds the March 2017 and November 2021 private medical opinions and June 2020 VA opinion establish that the Veteran's OSA is proximately due to the Veteran's decreased activity and obesity caused by service-connected PTSD, bilateral pes planus, and bilateral shoulder disabilities. See 38 C.F.R. § 3.310. The private physicians established that the Veteran's obesity, as an intermediate disorder caused by the Veteran's service-connected PTSD and musculoskeletal conditions, was a substantial factor to the Veteran's current diagnosis of OSA. See Walsh v. Wilkie, 32 Vet. App. 300, 305-07 (2020). The Veteran's private physicians provided opinions based on thorough reviews of the Veteran's medical treatment records and supported with citations to medical literature. Thus, the Board finds that the March 2017 and November 2021 examinations documenting the nature and etiology of the Veteran's OSA to be the most probative evidence of record. See Prejean v. West, 13 Vet. App. 444 (2000).

The Board acknowledges the negative nexus opinions provided by the Veteran's VA examinations, regarding whether the Veteran's PTSD proximately caused the Veteran's diagnosis of OSA. However, the Board finds that the evidence of record is at least in relative equipoise on this matter. When there is an approximate balance of positive and negative evidence regarding any issue material to the determination of a matter, by law, the Board must resolve all reasonable doubt in favor of the Veteran. See 38 U.S.C. § 5107; 38 C.F.R. § 3.102; see also Lynch v. McDonough, 21 F.4th 776 (Fed. Cir. 2021).

Thus, the benefit of the doubt must be resolved in favor of the Veteran, and entitlement to service connection for the Veteran's OSA condition secondary to his service-connected conditions is granted.

Citation Nr: 22001860

Entitlement to service connection for obstructive sleep apnea and type II diabetes mellitus is granted.

The Veteran contends that he has obstructive sleep apnea and type II diabetes mellitus which are caused or aggravated by his service-connected acquired psychiatric disability, to include as a result of weight gain and inactivity caused by that disability.

Service connection is established on a direct basis when there is competent, credible evidence of (1) a current disability, (2) in-service incurrence or aggravation of an injury or disease, and (3) a nexus, or link, between the current disability and the in-service disease or injury. 38 U.S.C. §§ 1110, 1131; Holton v. Shinseki, 557 F.3d 1363, 1366 (Fed. Cir. 2009); 38 C.F.R. § 3.303 (a), (d).

Service connection may be granted on a secondary basis for a disability that is proximately due to a service-connected condition. 38 C.F.R. § 3.310 (a). Service connection is also possible when a service-connected condition has aggravated a claimed condition, but compensation is only payable for the degree of additional disability attributable to the aggravation.

Allen v. Brown, 7 Vet. App. 439 (1995). In October 2006, VA amended 38 C.F.R. § 3.310 to incorporate the decision in Allen except that VA will not concede aggravation unless there is medical evidence showing the baseline level of the disability before its aggravation by the service-connected disability. 38 C.F.R. § 3.310 (b).

Obesity may serve as an "intermediate step" between a service-connected disability and a current disability that may be connected on a secondary basis. 38 C.F.R. § 3.310; see also Walsh v. Wilkie, 32 Vet. App. 300 (2020).

VA treatment records throughout the claims period note diagnosis with type II diabetes mellitus and obstructive sleep apnea.

In a December 2008 VA treatment record, reasons given by the Veteran for his overweight/obesity included "eating because of emotions or stress." His barriers to physical activity included "feeling bad about myself ... illness or injury" and "medications led to weight gain."

On VA examination in October 2010 the Veteran reported chronic sleep disturbance dating back to military service. He noted that he often went days without sleeping and had troubling dreams and nightmares. He reported typically sleeping 2-4 hours a day. He stated that it was often difficult to sleep because "there are spirits around me, the house is haunted, I'm going to move as soon as possible." The examiner noted that his sleep disturbance was further dysregulated by having diagnosed obstructive sleep apnea. The examiner rendered diagnoses of psychotic disorder, not otherwise specified, and personality disorder traits.

In a February 2012 VA treatment record, a VA physician stated that the Veteran's blood sugar was not well controlled "partly from antipsychotic medication."

On VA examination in May 2012 the Veteran was diagnosed with a psychotic disorder, not otherwise specified. The examiner noted that the Veteran had chronic sleep impairment and reported recurrent nightmares approximately 4 to 5 times per week.

An October 2014 letter from Dr. J.J.V. of Atlantis Health Services stated that the Veteran had been under that doctor's care for major depression and PTSD, and had a history of diabetes, sleep apnea, and hyperlipidemia. That physician stated that it was his medical opinion that the Veteran had symptoms of these conditions "due to all the bad experiences that he went through during his time in the active service, therefore they are connected." In a psychiatric evaluation report attached to the letter and dated June 2013, the physician reported that the Veteran had PTSD and probable generalized anxiety disorder. The Veteran's PTSD with major depression and sleep apnea were reportedly caused by his brother's death while he was in service as well as the assault he suffered in January 1983.

The Veteran testified at a June 2017 videoconference hearing that his diabetes was caused by the shock and fright he experienced as a result of his alleged in-service assault, and that his obstructive sleep apnea was caused by his service-connected psychiatric disorder.

In May 2019 a VA examiner opined that the claimed obstructive sleep apnea was less likely than not due to or the result of the Veteran's service-connected psychiatric disorder. The rationale was that obstructive sleep apnea was a condition known to be secondary to intermittent relaxation of the throat muscles blocking the airway during sleep. Known risk factors for obstructive sleep apnea included being overweight, and the Veteran weighed 191 lbs. at the time of testing and was 67 inches tall.

The May 2019 examiner also opined that the claimed diabetes mellitus was less likely than not secondary to an acquired psychiatric disorder. The rationale was that there was no pathophysiologic explanation for diabetes mellitus to be secondary to the psychiatric disorder. The examiner noted that one factor in the development of diabetes was being overweight, because in the presence of more fatty tissue, cells became more resistant to insulin.

In August 2021, a VA examiner opined that it was less likely than not that obstructive sleep apnea and type II diabetes mellitus were caused or aggravated by a service-connected acquired psychiatric disorder. The examiner reasoned that diabetes mellitus and obstructive sleep apnea were not medically related to the service-connected psychiatric disability, and that peer-reviewed evidence could not be found to support such a relationship. The examiner further opined that obesity was unrelated to the Veteran's acquired psychiatric disorder, again reasoning that obesity was not medically related to the service-connected psychiatric disability, and that peer-reviewed evidence could not be found to support such a relationship.

The August 2021 VA examiner failed to discuss the evidence of record supporting a relationship between the Veteran's psychiatric symptoms and obesity, nor did the examiner comment on the article Diabetes and Psychiatric Disorders, the October 2010 VA examination or the October 2014 private physician's opinion as explicitly required by the July 2021 Board remand. The August 2021 VA opinion is therefore inadequate. Stegall v. West, 11 Vet. App. 268, 271 (1998).

Based on the foregoing, the Board finds that the evidence is approximately balanced as to whether the Veteran's obstructive sleep apnea and type II diabetes mellitus were caused or aggravated by his service-connected acquired psychiatric disorder. Notably, the evidence above supports a plausible medical relationship between these disorders, to include as a result of weight gain and inactivity due to psychiatric symptoms or due to psychiatric medication. The October 2014 private opinion of Dr. J.J.V. constitutes competent evidence which appears to support this theory. While the VA examinations of record are against the claim, they are supported by inadequate rationale and afforded low probative value. Thus, while the October 2014 opinion of Dr. J.J.V. is unsupported by any extensive rationale, it is corroborated by the other evidence of record discussed above, to include the December 2008 VA treatment record noting that psychiatric symptoms contributed to inactivity and weight gain, and the February 2012 VA treatment record noting that psychiatric medication impaired blood sugar control. Thus, the evidence of record is in approximate balance.

As the evidence of record is in approximate balance as to whether current obstructive sleep apnea and type II diabetes mellitus are caused or aggravated by the Veteran's service-connected acquired psychiatric disorder, service connection is granted on this basis.

Citation Nr: 22020009

This matter was most recently before the Board in May 2020. At that time, the Board denied his claim for entitlement to service connection for obstructive sleep apnea. The Veteran subsequently appealed the Board's decision to the Court of Appeals for Veterans' Claims (the Court). In September 2021, the Court issued a memorandum decision, vacating the Board's decision as to this issue and remanding the claim due to the Board's failure to provide an adequate statement of reasons and bases for its decision. The claim is now back before the Board for adjudication.

In its May 2020 decision, the Board observed that the Veteran's service treatment records (STRs) were silent for complaints, diagnoses, or treatment for sleep apnea or its symptoms. In pertinent part, the Board assigned "significant weight" to the opinion presented alongside an August 2019 VA examination, which noted that the Veteran's BMI increased from 30 to 39 between 2007 and 2019 a significant finding since the strongest risk of sleep apnea is obesity. Additionally, the examiner observed that while some psychiatric medications have a known risk of weight gain, the Veteran's prescribed psychotropics did not belong to this category.

The Court found in its September 2021 memorandum decision that the August 2019 opinion was inadequate and therefore the Board decision was flawed by relying on its rationale. Specifically, the Court noted,

"There is evidence in the record that appears to contradict both the examiner's statement that [A]ppellant's medications were not in a class associated with weight gain as well as the Board's conclusion that none of the [A]ppellant's medical providers associated his psychiatric medications with weight gain."

In particular, the VA clinic records included a May 2015 progress note stating as follows:

At last visit, discontinued Mirtazipine, thought it remained on his last at his request in case he found he had difficulties. He initially stopped if after our last visit, but started back on it in the past week because he had "strange thoughts" along the lines of someone being in his house, feeling anxious. It also helps him to sleep. He realizes that it contributes to weight gain, but he is accepting of that issue at this time.

The Court determined that the Board's failure to consider this evidence the progress note was in error and a remand was necessary.

After remand by the Court, the Veteran has submitted additional evidence in support of his claim. One medical article notes that many patients, when exposed to psychotropic medications, gain significant weight. Other studies posit a relationship between sleep disruption and obesity, psychological factors, as well as a link between PTSD and obesity.

The Board finds that the evidence is at least in equipoise as to whether the Veteran's OSA is related to a service-connected disability. In that regard, the law is clear. Pursuant to the "benefit-of-the-doubt" rule, where there is "an approximate balance of positive and negative evidence regarding the merits of an issue material to the determination of the matter," the Veteran shall prevail upon the issue. 38 U.S.C. § 5107. The Board acknowledges that there is some evidence against the claim. In that regard, an August 2019 noted that the strongest risk of sleep apnea is obesity, and acknowledged that some psychiatric medications have a known risk of weight gain. However, that examiner concluded that the Veteran did not take any medications which caused weight gain. On the other hand, the Veteran has been prescribed Mirtazapine for sleep impairment which the Veteran's treating VA physician advised the Veteran contributed to weight gain.

VA's Office of General Counsel (OGC) precedential opinion addressed questions regarding whether obesity may be considered a "disease" for the purposes of service connection under U.S.C. §§ 1110 and 1131. In that regard, VAOPGCPREC 1-2017 recognized that obesity may act as an "intermediate step" between a service-connected disability and a current disability that may be service-connected on a secondary basis under 38 C.F.R. § 3.310(a). Here, there is competent evidence that the Veteran's service-connected medications contribute to weight gain and his VA clinician discussed this side-effect when determining the cost-benefit of continuing this medication. The VA examiner opinion against the claim conceded that certain medications could contribute to weight gain, but did not specifically discuss the Mirtazapine prescription. Moreover, there are medical articles discussing that many patients, when exposed to psychotropic medications, gain significant weight and studies posited a relationship between sleep disruption and obesity, psychological factors, as well as a link between PTSD and obesity.

Based on the foregoing, the Board concludes that, with the benefit of the doubt resolved in the Veteran's favor, a grant of service connection for obstructive sleep apnea as secondary to service-connected disabilities is warranted. See Wise v. Shinseki, 26 Vet. App. 517, 531 (2014) ("By requiring only an 'approximate balance of positive and negative evidence'..., the nation, 'in recognition of our debt to our veterans,' has 'taken upon itself the risk of error' in awarding... benefits.")

Citation Nr: 22012663

Initially, the Board finds that the Veteran has been diagnosed with OSA. See e. g., April 2015 VA examination report; see also March 2011 polysomnographic study report from Priority Sleep Diagnostics.

Next, the Veteran has been service connected for various disabilities, including posttraumatic stress disorder (PTSD) with unspecified depressive disorder and anxiety, and residuals of prostate cancer. See March 2021 rating decision codesheet.

Upon review of the lay and medical evidence of record, the Board finds that the evidence is at least in equipoise as to whether the Veteran's OSA is aggravated by his service-connected psychiatric and prostate cancer disabilities.

The evidence includes an April 2015 VA sleep apnea

examination report. During the evaluation, the Veteran specifically indicated that he was "unable to sleep due to having nightmares." He also indicated that he "can't stay asleep due to these nightmares & then he has trouble going back to sleep." The examiner opined that the Veteran's difficulty sleeping related to nightmares was not sleep apnea, but more likely than not related to insomnia. An opinion by the examiner as to whether the Veteran's OSA was aggravated by the nightmares (i. e., a symptom of a service-connected disability) was not provided.

Although a specific opinion as to aggravation was not provided by the April 2015 VA examiner, the Board finds that the opinion rendered weighs in favor of the claim. In this regard, the examiner specifically indicated that the Veteran's nighttime awaking and interrupted sleep was not due to OSA, but instead, was a result of a symptom associated with his service-connected psychiatric disability   (i. e., nightmares). In other words, the Veteran's sleep appeared to be interrupted both by his OSA and his nightmares. The examiner also indicated that "sleep apnea causes deprivation of quality of sleep." The Board finds it reasonable that interrupted sleep from nightmares (resulting in difficulty staying asleep and returning to sleep) likely would result in further "deprivation of sleep quality."

An April 2015 VA prostate cancer VA examination report further indicated that the Veteran's prostate cancer residuals resulted in "nighttime awakening to void 3 to 4 times" per night.

The evidence also includes a February 2016 VA psychiatric examination. At that time, the Veteran reported having nightmares of his service in Vietnam and indicated that he experienced nightmares approximately 4 times a week. This was noted to result in the Veteran sleeping only 3 hours per night. He also reported trouble with falling asleep and staying asleep. Most mornings, the Veteran stated that he felt "drowsy, tired." The examiner confirmed that the Veteran's psychiatric disability resulted in "sleep disturbance" and "chronic sleep impairment."

During a January 2016 VA mental health note, the Veteran reported symptoms of PTSD, depression, anxiety, sleep disturbance (sleeping 3-4 hrs a night) and nightmares.

In a recent August 2021 VA sleep apnea examination report, the Veteran again reported that, due to nightmares, he "could not sleep well."

A VA medical opinion was obtained in August 2021 pertaining to secondary service connection. In addressing the theory of aggravation, the examiner stated that the Veteran's "acquired psychiatric condition to include posttraumatic stress disorder and unspecified depressive disorder (claimed as PTSD, anxiety, and depression) and OSA are not connected in anyway and therefore cannot aggravate beyond its natural progression."

The Board finds that this opinion lacks probative value for several reasons. First, the examiner provided only a conclusory statement without a supporting rationale. See Miller v. West, 11 Vet. App. 345, 348 (1998) (a bare conclusion, even one reached by a health care professional, is not probative without a factual predicate in the record). Moreover, while the examiner indicated that aggravation beyond the natural progression was not shown, such is not required. See Ward v. Wilkie, 31 Vet. App. 233, 239 (2019) (permanent worsening is not a requirement for secondary service connection of a non-service-connected injury or disease). Further, the examiner did not address the Veteran's specific symptoms associated with his service-connected psychiatric disability, which includes nightmares. The evidence of record, as discussed above, clearly indicates that the Veteran's nightmares have impacted his ability to have uninterrupted sleep. For these reasons, the August 2021 VA medical opinion lacks probative value.

In sum, the Board finds that the Veteran's service-connected psychiatric and prostate cancer disabilities have served as an aggravating factor to his sleep apnearesulting in additional deprivation of his sleep quality. The Veteran has competently and credibly reported that, as a result of his nightmares (associated with his service-connected psychiatric disability), he has experienced increased nighttime awaking and difficulty retuning to sleep. His prostate cancer residuals, which include nighttime awakenings to void 3 to 4 times per night, would reasonably and additionally aggravate his sleep quality. As noted above, for secondary service connection, "aggravation" need not be permanent in nature. See Ward, 31 Vet. App. 241-42.

For these reasons, and resolving reasonable doubt in the Veteran's favor, the Board finds the criteria to establish service connection for OSA as secondary to the service-connected psychiatric and prostate cancer disabilities are met. 38 U.S.C. § 510 (b); 38 C.F.R. § 3.102. The appeal is granted.

Citation Nr: 22019768

Affording the Veteran the benefit of doubt, the evidence of record is approximately balanced ("nearly equal") in favor of finding the Veteran's currently diagnosed obstructive sleep apnea (See August 2017 VA examination which noted first diagnosis in 1996) is secondary to his other service-connected disabilities because his obstructive sleep apnea was either caused, in part, or aggravated by his service-connected disabilities due to an increase in weight and body fat brought on by the symptoms associated with his service-connected disabilities. Specifically, the Board finds the Veteran's testimony and statements are competent and credible evidence of symptoms, in some form, related to sleep apnea in service and his lack of desire to exercise due to pain caused from his service-connected musculoskeletal disabilities and lack of motivation caused by his PTSD. The Board finds that, although the VA examinations and medical opinions of record present negative causal link opinions, when considering all of these medical opinions as a whole, they support the Veteran's assertion that 1) he is service connected for many disabilities which have contributed to his weight gain and 2) obesity is a major cause, risk factor, or aggravation of his sleep apnea. To name a few for example, a July 2012 VA treatment record notes that the Veteran was identified as "at risk" for obesity related conditions, which included, among others, sleep apnea; a June 2015 VA treatment record noted the Veteran stated he could not walk very far because of his service-connected knee surgery, leg operation, and reported poor balance and falls; an April 2021 VA medical examiner stated that obesity is the leading risk factor in the development of obstructive sleep apnea due to neck fat obstructing the upper airway and opined that the Veteran's obese body habitus provides the most likely etiology for his obstructive sleep apnea. However, the Board affords the negative causal link VA opinions less probative value because they fail to adequately address the crux of the question at hand with adequate reasons and rationale, which has resulted in numerous remands as noted below. The Board finds those opinions do not persuasively refute the aforementioned evidence indicating observable symptoms of sleep apnea did significantly worsen due to the Veteran's obesity brought on, at least in part, by his service-connected disabilities. The Board notes that this finding is specific to the facts of this case with the specific medical evidence of this case showing a causal relationship between the Veteran's disabilities and associated symptoms, increasing weight, and the development or worsening of sleep apnea symptoms. The Board has reviewed all evidence in the claims file, with an emphasis on the evidence relevant to these appeals. Although the Board has an obligation to provide reasons and bases supporting its decision, there is no need to discuss, in detail, every piece of evidence of record. Gonzales v. West, 218 F.3d 1378, 1380-81 (Fed. Cir. 2000). Accordingly, service connection for obstructive sleep apnea is warranted.

Citation Nr: 22024573

Secondary service connection may be warranted for a current disability that is either proximately caused by or aggravated by a service-connected disability. 38 C.F.R. § 3.310(a), (b); Allen v. Brown, 7 Vet. App. 439 (1995). A "permanent worsening" of a non-service-connected disability is not required to establish secondary service connection on the basis of aggravation (i.e., aggravation may include temporary worsening of a disability). Ward v. Wilkie, 31 Vet. App. 233 (2019).

The Veteran generally contends that his OSA is secondary to (aggravated by) his service-connected PTSD. See February 2014 Correspondence.

Service treatment records do not document any pertinent OSA abnormalities upon entrance to, during, or upon separation from service. See September 1964, October 1966, July 1967, September 1968, April 1969, and February 1970 records.

A December 2013 Sanford Pulmonary and Sleep Medicine record documented the Veteran's diagnosis of OSA after a polysomnogram.

An October 2014 VA examiner rendered an unfavorable etiological opinion; however, as the November 2017 Board Decision found that opinion to be inadequate, the Board will not discuss it further herein.

In a November 2014 Sanford Pulmonary and Sleep Medicine record, the provider opined that, although the Veteran was likely to have suffered from OSA prior to developing PTSD, medical literature documents that PTSD makes the use of CPAP difficult and is a risk factor for CPAP failure; the provider further opined that the Veteran had a bidirectional relationship between his OSA and PTSD.

In a February 2015 Notice of Disagreement (NOD), a September 2015 VA Form 9, and an October 2017 Brief, the Veteran reiterated his belief that his OSA was secondary to his PTSD and cited supporting medical literature.

In a November 2017 private opinion, Dr. PS opined that the Veteran's OSA was aggravated by his PTSD because: (a) PTSD causes chronic activation of stress hormones (hypothalamic-pituitary-adrenal axis activity) which is known to lead to a neural sensitization leading to upper airway dysfunction such as OSA; and (b) nightmares related to PTSD also cause rapid breathing and gasping aggravating sleep apnea.

In a November 2017 private treatment record, Dr. GC opined that the Veteran's PTSD more likely than not aggravates his OSA as evidenced by PTSD symptoms (thrashing around, hypervigilance, and nightmares) which cause worsening of OSA severity, reducing his quality of sleep, and causing daytime sleepiness, irritability, and labile mood; the provider further noted that he confirms the evidence-based relationship between PTSD and OSA and provided citations to supporting medical literature.

In May 2018, the Veteran submitted several pieces of medical literature regarding the medical relationship between OSA and PTSD.

An April 2019 VA examiner rendered an unfavorable etiological opinion; however, as the December 2021 Court JMR found that opinion to be inadequate, the Board will not discuss it further herein.

Although all VA etiological opinions of record are inadequate, the Board finds that further remand is unnecessary because the private medical evidence of record is probative and sufficient to grant the claim. Specifically, the November 2014 record, the November 2017 opinion by Dr. PS, and the November 2017 record by Dr. GC are probative because the providers considered the Veteran's specific medical history, provided thorough rationale to support their conclusions, and also cited to ample medical literature in support of their opinions that the Veteran's OSA and its treatment with CPAP was at least as likely as not aggravated by his PTSD. Stefl v. Nicholson, 21 Vet. App. 120, 123-24 (2007) (finding that an adequate opinion is one that is based upon consideration of the Veteran's prior medical history and examinations, describes the disability in sufficient detail, and includes a conclusion supported by an analysis that the Board can consider and weigh against contrary opinions). Thus, the Board grants the claim on a secondary basis, resolving it in full.

Citation Nr: A22002044

The Veteran has contended that his sleep apnea is related to his active service. Alternatively, the Veteran has asserted that his sleep apnea is secondary to service-connected disabilities, to specifically include posttraumatic stress disorder (PTSD) and tinnitus.

In the October 2020 rating decision, the RO determined that the Veteran had been diagnosed with OSA. Additionally, the RO found that there was an in-service incurrence of OSA, to include a complaint of sleep disturbance at the Veteran's post-deployment health assessment in August 2006. The Board is bound by those favorable findings. 38 C.F.R. § 3.104(c) (2020).

Service treatment records (STRs) further documented that the Veteran was diagnosed with a sleep disorder in January 2006.

Regardless, the Veteran has reported that he first experienced symptoms associated with sleep apnea while he was in active service and that those symptoms have continued since that time. Heuer v. Brown, 7 Vet. App. 379 (1995); Falzone v. Brown, 8 Vet. App. 398 (1995); Caldwell v. Derwinski, 1 Vet. App. 466 (1991). Moreover, the Board finds the Veteran to be credible in that respect.

Additionally, the Veteran submitted statements from fellow service members and his wife describing the in-service onset and continuity of his symptoms since active service, to include trouble falling and staying asleep, snoring, and difficulty breathing while sleeping. The Board finds that laypersons are competent to establish the presence of observable symptomatology. Layno v. Brown, 6 Vet. App. 465 (1994). Furthermore, the Board finds the lay statements credible.

In October 2020, the Veteran was afforded a VA examination. The examiner opined that the Veteran's OSA was less likely than not incurred in or caused by his active service. The examiner acknowledged the lay statements of record but found no empirical objective diagnostic findings to support a diagnosis of OSA while on active duty. The examiner noted that the Veteran was not diagnosed with OSA until 2018, nine years post-service. The examiner explained the occurrence of OSA and stated that adding additional information to include the specific peer reviewed literature, will not change the outcome of the medical opinion.

The Board finds that the October 2020 VA medical opinion is inadequate for adjudication purposes. In this regard, the examiner did not address the in-service diagnosis for a sleep disorder and favorable finding of a complaint of sleep disturbance during service. Furthermore, the examiner did not consider the Veteran's competent and credible statements regarding the in-service onset and continuity of his symptoms since service.

Also of record is a January 2021 private medical opinion, added to the record in June 2021, during the 90-day period following the Veteran's May 2021 hearing before the Board. In that opinion, Dr. D.A. opined that it was at least as likely as not that the Veteran's sleep apnea was caused or aggravated by his service-connected PTSD and/or tinnitus. In so finding, Dr. D.A. cited to, and discussed, a wealth of medical literature in support of the appeal. Dr. D.A. concluded that based on a review of the literature, both PTSD and tinnitus on their own were sufficient to cause sleep apnea, and so, clearly a combination of both will cause sleep apnea. Dr. D.A. specifically noted that the scientific observation that the derangement of rapid eye movement (REM) sleep prominent in patients with PTSD was the cause for sleep apnea was of particular importance in this Veteran's case. In preparation of the medical opinion, Dr. D.A. noted that he reviewed the Veteran's claims file, reviewed the relevant medical literation, and interviewed the Veteran. Dr. D.A. noted that a physical examination of the Veteran was not performed, but would not have yielded any information as to the relationship between the Veteran's service-connected PTSD and tinnitus and his sleep apnea.

The Board finds that the January 2021 private medical opinion is adequate. In this regard, the examiner thoroughly reviewed and discussed the relevant evidence and medical literature, considered the contentions of the Veteran, and provided a supporting rationale for the conclusions reached. Barr v. Nicholson, 21 Vet. App. 303 (2007); Stefl v. Nicholson, 21 Vet. App. 120 (2007); Nieves-Rodriguez v. Peake, 22 Vet. App. 295 (2008). As such, the January 2021 private medical opinion is the most probative evidence of record concerning the Veteran's claim of entitlement to service connection for sleep apnea.

In sum, the Veteran has competently and credibly reported that his OSA had its onset during his active service and has continued since that time. The Veteran's fellow service members and wife corroborated his statements. Furthermore, there is a private medical opinion of record that weighs in favor of the Veteran's claim.

Citation Nr: 22023489

1. Service connection for obstructive sleep apnea

The Veteran seeks service connection for sleep apnea to include on a secondary basis.

Service connection is warranted where the evidence of record establishes that a particular injury or disease resulting in disability was incurred in the line of duty in the active military service or, if pre-existing such service, was aggravated thereby. 38 U.S.C. §§ 1110, 1131; 38 C.F.R. § 3.303(a).

To establish a right to compensation for a present disability, a veteran must show (1) the existence of a present disability; (2) in-service incurrence or aggravation of a disease or injury; and (3) a causal relationship, or nexus, between the present disability and the disease or injury incurred or aggravated during service. Shedden v. Principi, 381 F.3d 1163, 1167 (Fed. Cir. 2004).

A disability that is proximately due to, or results from, another disease or injury for which service connection has been granted shall be considered a part of the original condition. 38 C.F.R. § 3.310(a). Secondary service connection on the basis of aggravation is permitted under 38 C.F.R. § 3.310(b), and compensation is payable for that degree of aggravation of a non-service-connected disability caused by a service-connected disability and not due to the natural progress of the nonservice-connected disease. Allen v. Brown, 7 Vet. App. 439 (1995).

The Veteran is seeking service connection for sleep apnea. A February 2015 polysomnogram reflects that the Veteran has been diagnosed with obstructive sleep apnea.

In a January 2020 record opinion, Dr. R.N. opined that there was no more likely cause for the onset of the Veteran's sleep apnea than weight gain precipitated by his service-connected orthopedic and mental health conditions. Dr. R.N. further opined that the Veteran's obstructive sleep apnea was very likely caused primarily as a result of weight gain precipitated by his service-connected orthopedic and mental health conditions, and that therefore, it was very likely that the Veteran's obstructive sleep apnea was secondary to his active military service. Dr. R.N.'s opinion included a very lengthy discussion of pertinent medical literature and the facts of the Veteran's specific case. Further, Dr. Haines noted that he had reviewed the Veteran's claims file and treatment records.

There are no other opinions of record that address the secondary service connection theory. Therefore, the Board finds that service connection for sleep apnea as secondary to weight gain precipitated by his service-connected orthopedic and mental health conditions, is warranted.

Citation Nr: 22006336

The Veteran contends that his obstructive sleep apnea is secondary to his service-connected coronary artery disease and PTSD with cannabis use disorder.

Service connection may be granted for disability resulting from disease or injury incurred in or aggravated by active service. 38 U.S.C. §§ 1110, 5107; 38 C.F.R. § 3.303. The three-element test for service connection requires evidence of: (1) a current disability; (2) in-service incurrence or aggravation of a disease or injury; and (3) a causal relationship between the current disability and the in-service disease or injury. Shedden v. Principi, 381 F.3d 1163, 1166 -67 (Fed. Cir. 2004). Service connection may also be granted for a disability that is proximately due to, or aggravated by, service-connected disease or injury. 38 C.F.R. § 3.310.

In August 2021, the Veteran submitted a Sleep Apnea Disability Benefits Questionnaire and opinion prepared by M. Blevins, M.D. In her opinion, Dr. Blevins finds that it is at least as likely as not that the Veteran's service-connected PTSD with cannabis abuse has caused and continues to aggravate his obstructive sleep apnea. As a rationale for that opinion, she explains that marijuana may be classified as a stimulant, hallucinogen, or depressant depending upon the type of marijuana and the psychological and physical effects it has on the individual. In the Veteran's case, he is consistently noted as using marijuana to self-medicate based on its sedating effects, which he has stated relax him and help him to sleep. Dr. Blevins further cites to medical literature showing that sedative drugs suppress the central nervous system, which is typically accompanied by a reduction in carbon dioxide responsiveness in the medullary respiratory center, loss of airway control, and respiratory depression. Because breathing is paused or shallow during sleep with sleep apnea, the introduction of a drug that results in respiratory pauses, irregular breathing, and shallow breaths increases the risk for harmful respiratory events. Dr. Blevins further agreed with a March 2018 private examiner who found that the Veteran's obstructive sleep apnea is caused by his obesity. The Veteran reported during the consultation portion of the examination with Dr. Blevins that he often eats when he is stressed and that, due to his service-connected coronary artery disease, he has limited ability to participate in exercise activity. Therefore, his obesity has acted as an intermediate step between his service-connected PTSD with cannabis abuse and coronary artery disease and his obstructive sleep apnea. The Board finds that Dr. Blevins's opinion is entitled to probative weight because it was provided based on an accurate understanding of the Veteran's medical history, both as presented in the record and in the consultation portion of her examination, and because it is supported by appropriate rationale. See Nieves-Rodriguez v. Peake, 22 Vet. App. 295 (2008); Prejean v. West, 13 Vet. App. 444 (2000).

On the other hand, an April 2021 VA examiner opined that the Veteran's obstructive sleep apnea is less likely than not proximately due to, the result of, or aggravated by his service-connected disabilities. As a rationale for that opinion, the examiner explained that obstructive sleep apnea is due to obstruction in the upper airways, which is a mechanical/anatomical finding. Depression and anxiety do not lead to this obstruction. In addition, the Veteran is considered obese, which is the cause of his obstructive sleep apnea. The Board finds no reason to afford greater weight to the April 2021 VA examiner's negative opinion than to Dr. Blevins's positive opinion because the VA examiner did not address the cannabis abuse aspect of the Veteran's service-connected psychiatric disability and did not address whether the Veteran's obesity may be an intermediate step between his service-connected disabilities and his obstructive sleep apnea.

Accordingly, the Board finds that the evidence is at least in approximate balance as to whether the Veteran's obstructive sleep apnea is secondary to his service-connected disabilities, particularly his PTSD with cannabis abuse and his service-connected coronary artery disease. The benefit of the doubt is resolved in the Veteran's favor, and the Board therefore concludes that entitlement to service connection for obstructive sleep apnea must be granted. 38 U.S.C. § 5107(b); 38 C.F.R. § 3.102.

Citation Nr: 22016857

The claim of entitlement to service connection for OSA, to include as secondary to a service-connected condition.

The Veteran contends that his sleep apnea was caused or aggravated by his active military service.

Service connection may be granted for disability resulting from disease or injury incurred in or aggravated by active service. 38 U.S.C. §§ 1110, 1131, 5107; 38 C.F.R. § 3.303. The three-element test for service connection requires evidence of: (1) a current disability; (2) in-service incurrence or aggravation of a disease or injury; and (3) a causal relationship between the current disability and the in-service disease or injury. Shedden v. Principi, 381 F.3d 1163, 1166 -67 (Fed. Cir. 2004).

When there is an approximate balance of positive and negative evidence regarding any issue material to the determination of a matter, the Secretary shall give the benefit of the doubt to the claimant. 38 U.S.C. § 5107(b). The benefit-of-the-doubt rule applies if the competing evidence is "nearly equal" or in "approximate balance." This rule does not apply when the evidence persuasively favors one side or the other. See Lynch v. McDonough, 21 F.4th 776 (Fed. Cir. 2021) (en banc).

In this case, the Board concludes that the Veteran has a current disability that began during active service in connection with his allergic rhinitis. 38 U.S.C. §§ 1110, 1131, 5107(b); Holton v. Shinseki, 557 F.3d 1363, 1366 (Fed. Cir. 2009); 38 C.F.R. § 3.303(a).

The evidence of record confirms that the Veteran has a current diagnosis of obstructive sleep apnea. See, e.g., November 2015 VA medical opinion; February 2019 private opinion. As such, the first element of service connection is met.

Next, while the Veteran's service treatment records (STRs) do not contain specific complaint or diagnosis of sleep apnea, one May 1990 record indicates that he was assessed with an overdose of caffeine due to taking multiple caffeine tablets. A November 1989 record indicates that the Veteran had problems breathing through his nose since boot camp. Additionally, a September 2014 lay statement from the Veteran's parent, who has the initials S.M., indicates that they first observed the Veteran snoring and taking deep breaths in his sleep after he began his active service, and that the Veteran reported he did not sleep well during his active service. Further, as outlined below, the Board finds that the Veteran's service-connected allergic rhinitis, which had its onset in service, is a significant contributing factor in the onset and development of the Veteran's current OSA. See August 2013 rating decision; February 2019 private opinion of Dr. C.L.S.

Given this evidence of in-service symptomatology, the remaining question is whether the current disability is related to the Veteran's active service. On this question there are probative opinions in favor of and against the claim.

The evidence in favor of the claim includes a February 2019 private opinion letter and corresponding disability benefits questionnaire (DBQ) provided by a physician with the initials C.L.S. Dr. C.L.S. included in her letter a summary of her qualifications to provide the nexus opinion, noting, among other things, that she is a Board-Certified Sleep Specialist with over 30 years of experience in sleep medicine. Dr. C.L.S. explained, based on her expertise and research, that the "etiology of sleep apnea is quite complex and may include many different factors. The most important factors are the structure of the individual's airways, the presence of any chronic abnormalities of the upper airways, and the nature of the relaxation of the airways and the neck that occurs during sleep." Dr. C.L.S. stated that "[a]llergic rhinitis and nasal congestion are factors in the onset and worsening of snoring and sleep apnea" and stated that OSA develops slowly and worsens over time. Dr. C.L.S. also noted that allergic rhinitis is an abnormality of the upper airway that can cause chronic inflammation, swelling, irritation, and mouth breathing. Dr. C.L.S. cited recent research further showing that individuals with depression and PTSD, such as the Veteran, are more likely than other adults to have underlying, undiagnosed, and untreated sleep apnea.

Specific to the Veteran's case, Dr. C.L.S. opined that the Veteran's sleep apnea developed during the years of his active service, citing his long history of allergic rhinitis that began during active duty, his referral during service for ENT evaluation and treatment, and other characteristics identified in the Veteran's past sleep studies. The Board finds this opinion persuasive as C.L.S. expressly noted her review of the Veteran's service records and cited multiple recent medical studies in support of her conclusions. Dr. C.L.S. also addressed the conflicting conclusions made by the VA medical examiner, noting that the VA examiner's opinion was based on outdated research and that the examiner did not address the impact of the Veteran's rhinitis on the development of his OSA.

The evidence against the claim includes a VA medical opinion, which essentially attributes the Veteran's OSA to his weight. The Board finds this opinion lacks probative value as it fails to address the complexity of several other potentially causative factors of the Veteran's OSA, as clearly outlined by Dr. C.L.S. Further, the examiner failed to address whether the Veteran's allergic rhinitis or PTSD could cause or aggravate the Veteran's OSA, and the examiner failed to address the competent lay evidence of relevant symptoms of a sleep disorder during active service.

Upon review of the entire record, the Board finds the evidence to be in approximate balance as to whether the Veteran's current OSA is related to service. Accordingly, after resolving all doubt in favor of the Veteran, the Board finds that service connection for OSA is warranted. 38 U.S.C. § 5107; 38 C.F.R. § 3.102.

Citation Nr: A22004816

Service connection for OSA is granted

The Veteran's primary contention appears to be that his service-connected posttraumatic stress disorder (PTSD) medications and stressor events have contributed to significant weight gain of over 50 pounds, and that his weight gain caused his sleep apnea. See April 2016 Veteran's statement.

Service connection may be granted for a disability that is proximately due to, or aggravated by, service-connected disease or injury. 38 C.F.R. § 3.310. Per a 2017 VA General Counsel (G.C.) precedential opinion, obesity may be an "intermediate step" between a service-connected disability and a current disability that may be service connected on a secondary basis under 38 C.F.R. § 3.310 (a). See VAOPGCPREC 01-17 (Jan. 6, 2017), at 2-3. Service connection may be granted on a secondary basis where the claimed disability would not have occurred but for obesity caused or aggravated by a service-connected disability. Id.; 38 C.F.R. § 3.310. Walsh v. Wilkie, 32 Vet. App. 300 (2020).

Initially, a March 2016 private sleep study diagnosed moderate OSA. A May 2016 VA examiner provided a negative medical opinion on the possibility of secondary service connection for the Veteran's OSA as caused by and/or aggravated by his service-connected PTSD, and instead attributed OSA to weight gain after service. However, the examiner did not address whether the Veteran's service-connected PTSD and its medications aggravated his obesity. Thus, the May 2016 VA examiner's opinion was inadequate and entitled to limited probative value against the claim.

In contrast, there is highly probative medical opinion evidence in support of whether the Veteran's OSA was caused and/or aggravated by service-connected PTSD and its medications, with consideration of obesity as an intermediate step.

In particular, an August 2018 positive nexus opinion by M.B., PA-C, stated that OSA is secondary to, related to, and/or aggravated by service-connected PTSD with subsequent sleep disturbance and weight gain. Notably, based on a review of several cited medical articles and the Veteran's medical records, M.B. reasoned that "the risk of developing OSA as a result of PTSD is related to weight gain and obesity, and it is well-documented that PTSD predisposes an individual to weight gain." M.B. further reasoned, "Thus, this Veteran's mental health medications have contributed to weight gain as well as his sleep disturbances which, at the very least, aggravated his OSA condition."

Similarly, the March 2016 opinion and October 2016 addendum by G.U., Nurse Practitioner, discussed in detail the links between OSA and weight gain and PTSD, based on review of relevant medical literature, and opined that the Veteran's service-connected OSA condition was secondary to, related to, and/or aggravated by his service-connected PTSD and PTSD medication with weight gain. Further, an April 2019 addendum opinion by G.U. clarified that the Veteran's weight gain and obesity are due to and/or related to his service-connected PTSD. Altogether, the Board finds these private positive opinions to be probative and largely supported by the claims file, including relevant medical records, such as the August 2018 sleep apnea Disability Benefits Questionnaire (DBQ), the Veteran's lay statements, and medical literature, clinical expertise, and discussion of the rationale of the opinion. See Nieves-Rodriguez v. Peake, 22 Vet. App. 295 (2008) ("It is the factually accurate, fully articulated, sound reasoning for the conclusion, not the mere fact that the claims file was reviewed, that contributes probative value to a medical opinion.").

The approximate balance of the evidence is in favor of service connection for OSA on a secondary basis to the Veteran's service-connected PTSD. 38 U.S.C. § 5107 (b). Therefore, after resolving any doubt in the Veteran's favor, service connection for OSA is warranted.

HOW MANY STARS WOULD YOU GIVE THIS BOOK?

Please help other Veterans; leave a review to help them evaluate whether they should read this book or not. If you found this book helpful or even if you totally disagree with Dr. Finnerty, please help other Veterans by leaving feedback on Amazon and anywhere else relevant. How many stars should this book receive?